NEIGHBOURHOOD MANAGEMENT: A GOOD PRACTICE GUIDE

PETE DUNCAN AND SALLY THOMAS

CHARTERED INSTITUTE OF HOUSING
THE HOUSING CORPORATION
THE PLACES FOR PEOPLE GROUP

The Chartered Institute of Housing

The Chartered Institute of Housing is the professional organisation for all people who work in housing. Its purpose is to maximise the contribution that housing professionals make to the well-being of communities. The Institute has more than 17,000 members working in local authorities, housing associations, the private sector and educational institutions.

Chartered Institute of Housing
Octavia House
Westwood Way
Coventry
CV4 8JP
Tel: 024 7685 1700 Fax: 024 7669 5110
Website: www.cih.org

The Housing Corporation

The Housing Corporation is the government agency which registers, regulates and funds over 2,000 social landlords in England, which between them provide around 1.5 million homes for people in need. The Corporation has an important role as a promoter of good practice in the social housing sector.

The Housing Corporation
149 Tottenham Court Road
London W1P 0BN
Tel: 020 7393 2000   Fax: 020 7393 2111
Website: www.housingcorp.gov.uk

The Places for People Group

The Places for People Group is one of the country's leading housing providers. It is responsible for around 53,000 homes throughout the UK which include houses and flats for affordable rent through to the latest loft-style apartments for sale. The Group also provides a range of community-based services such as childcare, financial services and employment and training opportunities. Its member companies are NBH, New Leaf *supporting independence*, Blueroom Properties, PfP Developments, JVCo, Bristol Churches Housing Association, Edinvar Housing Association and Kush Housing Association.

Neighbourhood Management: A Good Practice Guide
Written by Pete Duncan and Sally Thomas
Commissioning editor: Jane Allanson
Editor: Marie Vernon
© Chartered Institute of Housing and the Housing Corporation 2001
ISBN: 1-903208-12-2

Design by Jeremy Spencer
Cover illustration by Liz Pichon
Printed by: Genesis Print and Marketing, Croydon

CONTENTS

FOREWORD

A message from Lord Falconer, Minister for Housing, Planning and Regeneration

Much has been written about the principles of Neighbourhood Management but little about what works in practice. Until now. This Guide seeks to plug the gap, giving communities and professionals real life examples of Neighbourhood Management successes.

It should be important reading for anyone with an interest in regenerating our most deprived communities. This is because successful neighbourhood management is at the very heart of our regeneration agenda.

We all know it it is a challenging agenda – and we all know it will take time to succeed. But its best chance of success lies with breaking down barriers to change, improving co-ordination, seeking new ways of governing by local authorities and fully involving the community at all stages of delivery.

We are at the start of a fundamental change in the way we tackle neighbourhood deprivation in England. It is in everyone's interest to make sure we succeed. This Guide should help.

Lord Falconer

About the Authors

Sally Thomas and **Pete Duncan** are partners in Social Regeneration Consultants. SRC is based in North East England. It specialises in community-based urban regeneration, working closely with local communities and regeneration agencies on a broad range of initiatives.

The authors have considerable experience of community-based urban regeneration and housing. They have worked for local authorities, housing associations and co-operatives, Government agencies, community groups and voluntary sector organisations, as employees, board members and consultants.

ACKNOWLEDGEMENTS

The Chartered Institute of Housing would like to thank the Housing Corporation for funding the research, writing and production of this Guide through its Innovation and Good Practice (IGP) Grant programme. Funding from the Places for People Group is also gratefully acknowledged.

The following people gave their time to read and comment on the text at various stages, and their feedback was invaluable:

Aaron Cahill	National Housing Federation
Atul Patel	ASRA Housing Association (formerly with the Neighbourhood Renewal Unit)
Barrington Billings	Housing Corporation
David Cowans	Places for People Group
Glyn Perrens	Chartered Institute of Housing
Iain Roxburgh	Coventry City Council
Jan Bird	Department for Transport, Local Government and the Regions
Jerry Le Seuer	East Brighton NDC/DTLR
Marilyn Taylor	University of Brighton
Mark Lupton	Chartered Institute of Housing
Maureen Adams	Housing Corporation
Melanie Rees	Chartered Institute of Housing
Paul Roberts	Cadarn Housing Group
Peter Chapman	HACAS Chapman Hendy
Phil Morgan	TPAS (England)
Roger Jarman	Audit Commission
Steve Robinson	Liverpool City Council
John Thornhill	Chartered Institute of Housing

Thanks are also due to the organisations and individuals which discussed the issues and initiatives surrounding Neighbourhood Management and provided good practice examples.

CHAPTER 1

❏ What is Neighbourhood Management?

Neighbourhood Management is essentially about joining up services at a local level and making them more relevant to people's lives. But it has a much broader context. It is one of the crucial tools in the process of re-drawing the relationship between the state, at central and local level, and the people. It is about changing the balance of power in our neighbourhoods, moving firmly away from the paternalism of the past to a new era of active, engaged communities.

The overall goal of Neighbourhood Management is to ensure the economic, social and political inclusion of disadvantaged areas and their residents, so that they have access to their full rights as citizens. Neighbourhood Management should therefore be a key contributor to the creation of a more civil, equitable and empowered society.

Neighbourhood Management is about much more than housing. It is about the organisation and delivery of the full range of local services. It is also about how these services meet the needs and expectations of the people who live in these neighbourhoods and their ability to have some control over how they are provided. It has relevance to rural as well as urban areas. The authors of this Guide have formed their own definition:

> *'Neighbourhood Management is a process which enables local communities to work with providers of neighbourhood services to meet local needs and expectations more effectively and in a way which secures and develops local accountability.'*

This deliberately places the emphasis on local communities, rather than service providers, whilst recognising the importance of a genuine partnership between them and the importance of effective 'joined up' delivery on the ground.

This distinction is important. Thirty years of urban renewal have had mixed success. The consensus amongst researchers and policy makers is that the missing ingredient in many cases has been sustained community ownership of both the delivery process and management of the outcomes. Put simply, Neighbourhood Management will not work unless local communities play a leading role. It is much more than improving the efficiency and co-ordination of local services.

❑ Neighbourhood Management – the key features

The ultimate aim of the Government's National Strategy for Neighbourhood Renewal is reducing the inequalities in the five key areas of housing and the physical environment, crime, health, education and jobs. It is about closing the social and economic gap between the most deprived areas and the rest of the country. Neighbourhood Management is central to this objective.

The Government's Social Exclusion Unit, set up in 1997, established 18 Policy Action Teams to carry out detailed work on the National Strategy. One of these, Policy Action Team 4, focused specifically on Neighbourhood Management. Its report, published in 2000, and the subsequent pathfinder bidding guidance from the Department for the Environment, Transport and the Regions (DETR) (now the Department for Transport, Local Government and the Regions (DTLR)), highlighted six key features of a successful Neighbourhood Management approach:

- Someone with overall responsibility at the neighbourhood level
- Community involvement at the outset
- The tools to get things done
- A systematic, planned approach to tackling problems
- Effective delivery mechanisms
- A commitment from service providers

In practice, this means that Neighbourhood Management, once fully established, should have a powerful neighbourhood manager, ideally responsible to some form of community-led Board, with authority over a wide range of neighbourhood services and with devolved budgets to ensure they can deliver Best Value for communities, not just providers.

It is important to recognise that Neighbourhood Management is a process, not a project; an approach to tackling neighbourhood renewal, but not a complete solution in itself; a way of delivering local services which, whilst initially focused on deprived communities, will almost certainly have relevance for all communities.

❑ Purpose of the Guide

The aim of this Guide is to provide housing professionals and others with an accessible and practical tool that explains how they can engage successfully with the Government's neighbourhood agenda in general, and Neighbourhood Management in particular.

Neighbourhood Management is in its infancy. Whilst there are a number of high profile initiatives which have been experimenting with aspects of Neighbourhood Management for some time, few, if any, can yet claim to have a comprehensive approach in place.

Elements of this approach are to be found in a variety of 'joined-up' initiatives established by a number of local authorities, registered social landlords (RSLs), Housing Action Trusts, tenant management organisations and community-based regeneration agencies. These elements include, amongst others:

- On-the-spot housing management
- Neighbourhood wardens and super-caretakers
- Neighbourhood or community forums
- Community-led management boards
- Community agreements
- Estate management agreements
- Area co-ordination initiatives
- Service level agreements
- Devolved service budgets

These are all potential ingredients of a comprehensive Neighbourhood Management approach, but they do not, in themselves, represent the whole picture. Many agencies are now beginning to explore how these and other elements of their work in neighbourhoods might best be joined together to deliver the right mix. Many local communities are beginning to recognise that they can take a leading role in managing their own neighbourhoods – that the days of complaining about poor local services may soon be replaced by a real ability to do something about it.

It will, however, be several years before it will be possible to evaluate the overall success of the Neighbourhood Management approach and write a definitive guide to good practice. There is simply not yet enough good practice around to make informed judgements about what works and what does not.

This Guide therefore seeks to point organisations in the right direction, drawing on relevant good practice where it can, but also on the authors' own experience and approaches in this field. The Guide does not therefore seek to be definitive. Indeed it would be wrong to be prescriptive about Neighbourhood Management. At least 69 pathfinder projects will be underway by late 2001. Each will have a different approach and there will be many lessons to be learned by those that follow. There will also be a range of other initiatives which will develop independently of the pathfinders.

This is very much the starting point for this Guide and for much of the detailed advice that follows.

❑ Who the Guide is for

This Guide is aimed primarily at housing professionals and others directly involved in the renewal and management of neighbourhoods. Engaging with the Government's neighbourhood agenda is important for all professions involved in the complex area of urban and rural regeneration, but for housing professionals it has particular relevance.

Housing organisations are usually the largest stakeholders in deprived neighbourhoods, often with extensive neighbourhood assets, local management arrangements and well-established consultation structures with local communities. For this reason, if no other, local authority housing departments and registered social landlords have a potentially major role to play in pioneering best practice in Neighbourhood Management.

Turning this potential into reality is crucially important for the profession, not least because there has been concern that housing has not been given sufficient weight within the development of the neighbourhood agenda.

The research for this Guide covered England only. However, the principles behind Neighbourhood Management are also likely to be applied in the other parts of the United Kingdom.

For instance, similar approaches within other parts of the UK include the Communities First programme in Wales which is designed to enable communities to pursue sustainable development and tackle social disadvantage locally in ways which best meet their needs. The pilot Locality Budgeting initiative in Scotland also has elements of the Neighbourhood Management approach within it.

❑ Structure of the Guide

The Guide begins with an analysis of where Neighbourhood Management sits within the broad strategic framework of neighbourhood renewal. It then explains how local communities can be fully engaged in the Neighbourhood Management process and what housing professionals can do to make sure it is successful and sustainable.

Subsequent chapters examine how housing organisations can build up their capacity to handle Neighbourhood Management, and the skills and knowledge they will need to make it happen.

The Guide also provides practical guidance on how Neighbourhood Management can be implemented, drawing on case study material from a variety of organisations with some experience of it. The Guide finishes with a chapter on the most effective ways of monitoring and evaluating the impact of Neighbourhood Management on local service delivery.

CHAPTER 2

THE BACKGROUND

___

What this Chapter is about

This chapter considers:

- The background to Neighbourhood Management and the thinking behind it
- The strategies for modernisation at central, regional, sub-regional and local level
- The implications for RSLs

In January 2001, the Government published an Action Plan setting out a National Strategy for Neighbourhood Renewal (NSNR). It was the result of a three year analysis of how to stop decline in the country's poorest neighbourhoods. It pulled together the work of 18 Policy Action Teams (PATs) which carried out detailed research on the issues affecting declining neighbourhoods. It set out an ambitious vision on the part of Government:

'that, within 10 to 20 years, no-one should be seriously disadvantaged by where they live. People on low incomes should not have to suffer conditions and services that are failing, and so different from what the rest of the population receives.'

Source: Social Exclusion Unit (2001b)

This change will be achieved through new national policies, funding and targets, better local co-ordination and community empowerment, and national and regional support. As a result, the National Strategy Action Plan proposes two long-term goals:

- All the poorest neighbourhoods are to have common goals of lower worklessness and crime, and better health, skills, housing and physical environment
- To narrow the gap (on these measures) between the most deprived neighbourhoods and the rest of the country

Neighbourhood Management was the subject of one of the Policy Action Team reports and emerged as a potential solution to the problems of deprived neighbourhoods. It is seen as one of the main *mechanisms* through which the gap will be narrowed. It will improve local services, making them more responsive and accountable to local needs, getting them to work better together, and ensuring they deliver locally-agreed priorities. In short, the vast amounts of money spent on public services will be spent to better effect. Neighbourhood Management is also an important part of the *process* through which better local co-ordination and community empowerment will be achieved.

Neighbourhood Management is not the only policy initiative which addresses public service delivery. Although Neighbourhood Management is only part of a broader agenda to modernise central, regional and local government, it is potentially the most significant in terms of impact.

There is a hierarchy of interlocking initiatives of which Local Strategic Partnerships and Neighbourhood Management form part of and can be summarised as follows:

The modernisation agenda – responsibilities and strategies

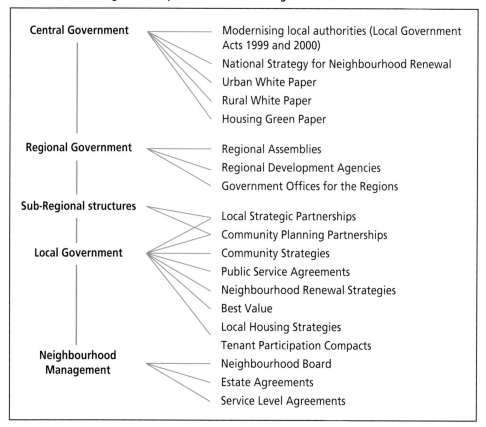

❏ Strategy for modernisation at Central Government level

On a wider canvas, the National Strategy for Neighbourhood Renewal and Neighbourhood Management are part of a comprehensive, strategic approach to urban and rural renewal.

The Urban and Rural White Papers set out the key principles of the Government's vision of renewal. That is, environmental improvement and sustainability, economic regeneration, empowering local communities and improving public services. New structures, a range of policies and programmes, and resources will be deployed in support of the overall aim of renewal. The aim is to establish and 'join up' structures at national, regional, local and community levels. Policies will accompany each structure and will provide a framework within which urban and rural renewal can be achieved.

The Housing Green Paper links closely with the broader social agenda within the two White Papers and paves the way for the re-positioning of housing as a key factor in achieving urban and rural regeneration. The key proposals relating to urban and rural renewal are outlined in Appendix 1.

The changes envisaged by the Green Paper will require local authorities and RSLs to work with their partners to develop, deliver and co-ordinate activities. This will be achieved through involvement in Local Strategic Partnerships (LSPs); consulting and empowering local communities, ensuring that housing strategies are responsive to local need; and improving service delivery. Following on from this, Neighbourhood Management will be expected to focus on the five key areas the Government has identified as priorities for achieving improvement. These are employment, education, health, crime, and housing and the physical environment. So it will need to focus on the range of problems people face in deprived areas and how these can be improved in an integrated way through the agencies which provide services locally.

❏ Strategy for modernisation at Regional Government level

At a regional level, strategies for modernisation can be found within the following:
- **Regional Assemblies** – the mechanism for delivering the regional view of the Regional Development Agencies (see below) i.e. a regional strategy. They are voluntary groups of councillors from local authorities, representatives from various sectors (i.e. business, education, training, the voluntary, cultural and environmental sectors including housing and health) with a stake in the region's economic, environmental and social well being.

- **Regional Development Agencies (RDAs)** – formally launched in April 1999. Their aim is to further economic development and regeneration, to promote business efficiency, investment and competitiveness to encourage employment and to contribute to sustainable development. This is achieved by formulating a regional strategy. Local authorities have a significant stake in the work of the RDA. They are accountable to Ministers and Parliament but also to anyone interested in their work at a regional level.
- **Government Offices for the Regions** have responsibilities for housing, planning and transport. Government Offices work closely with RDAs and take forward these responsibilities in the economic development and regeneration field.

❏ Strategy for modernisation at Sub-Regional level

At sub-regional level, strategies for modernisation can be found within the following:

Local Strategic Partnerships – Local Strategic Partnerships (LSPs) are one of the key elements in partnership working and Neighbourhood Management. They are intended to be the mechanism which will give the neighbourhood manager direction and support and ensure that the NSNR is delivered at a local level. They will be bodies that:

- Bring together at a local level the different parts of the public sector as well as the private, business, community and voluntary sectors so that different initiatives and services support each other and work together
- Are non-statutory and non-executive, i.e. they are not service deliverers
- Operate at a level which enables strategic decisions to be taken and is close enough to individual neighbourhoods to allow actions to be determined at community level
- Should be aligned with local authority boundaries

Their core tasks will be to:

- Prepare and implement a community strategy for the area (see later)
- Bring together local plans, partnerships and initiatives to provide a forum through which mainstream public service providers work together
- Devise targets for local public service agreements and to assist in their delivery
- Develop and deliver a local neighbourhood renewal strategy

Source: DETR (2001a)

Together with local communities, LSPs will determine priority neighbourhoods for Neighbourhood Management. They will provide neighbourhood managers with a route through which they can exercise influence over mainstream programme delivery, acting as troubleshooters if necessary.

While LSPs are only a requirement for the 88 areas eligible for Neighbourhood Renewal Fund (NRF) money, the duty to prepare community strategies effectively requires that an LSP is formulated in all authorities. While no single model will be imposed, or is likely to emerge, four scenarios may occur:

- Where nothing has been done – partnership is a token arrangement and everything will emanate from the local authority
- Where there is little or no regeneration funding – a partnership is developed to produce a community strategy and possibly qualify the area for future funding
- Where there is an existing partnership – it is likely to become an LSP
- Where there has been significant regeneration funding and/or the area qualifies for NRF – a glut of existing partnerships will have to be rationalised to develop an LSP and appropriate linkages

Source: Lipman, C (2001)

Community Planning Partnerships – Local authorities are required to produce a community strategy for promoting and improving the economic, social and environmental well being of their communities, through pooling budgets, joint commissioning of services and integrating service provision with other providers. In preparing community strategies local authorities will be required to consult and seek the participation of statutory, non-statutory and voluntary organisations that provide services. Local authorities are expected to ensure the commitment of other organisations by establishing community planning partnerships. That partnership should provide a voluntary framework for local co-operation.

❏ Strategy for modernisation at Local Government level

At local government level, strategies for modernisation can be found within the following:

Local Strategic Partnerships – (as above)

Community Planning Partnerships – (as above)

Community strategies set out the long-term vision for an area, provide an action plan and reflect the commitment and practical input of all the agencies and organisations which will assist in its delivery.

Public Service Agreements – Neighbourhood renewal depends on the successful operation of local public service agreements (local PSAs), partnership agreements between a local authority and the Government which are intended to improve outcomes in the six key areas more quickly and/or to a higher level than would otherwise be the case. The local authority receives a financial reward and the freedom to decide how best to deliver a particular service.

Local PSAs are currently being piloted in 20 local authorities. If successful, they will be rolled out nationally in the next two years to a further 130 areas.

Neighbourhood Renewal Strategies – Set out how improvements will be made in deprived neighbourhoods in the five key areas of employment, education, health, crime, and housing and physical environment which, in the 88 most deprived areas in England, will be supported by funding from the Neighbourhood Renewal Fund for three years.

Best Value – The modernisation agenda includes Best Value, one of the main ways in which councils and RSLs can structure and deliver a different way of working through reviewing the performance of all services systematically on a five year cycle. The intention is to continuously improve services and identify poor standards and performance through Best Value Performance Plans and Reviews .

Local Housing Strategies – Local authorities are required to put in place a planning and action framework for all organisations concerned with local housing. A comprehensive multi-disciplinary housing strategy is essential, covering all tenures and involving all partner agencies in order to secure a co-ordinated approach. Whilst local authorities take the lead in drawing up the strategy and putting it in place, the input of agencies such as housing associations, developers, private landlords, health authorities and social services departments must also be actively sought.

Tenant Participation Compacts – These are local authority wide agreements with tenants aimed at ensuring that they have a greater say in the management of their homes. They are now in place in virtually all local authorities, creating a more structured approach to tenant involvement. The best of them are highly innovative and are effectively acting as pilots for local public service agreements (see above) which will extend beyond housing services in the future.

❏ Strategies for modernisation at a local level

Neighbourhood Management is to be delivered in individual neighbourhoods, determined through the LSP in consultation with local communities. There are likely to be many models for Neighbourhood Management. Current initiatives which display elements of possible approaches are neighbourhood boards, Estate Agreements and service level agreements (see later).

❏ Strategies for modernisation at all levels

E-government initiatives are intended to provide channels of communication which support all elements of modernisation, through improving general access to public services

❏ What are the implications for RSLs?

For RSLs, the strategic framework outlined above has similarities and differences. The principles of Best Value and Tenant Participation Compacts have been extended to RSLs, although they are not currently statutory or regulatory requirements. The Housing Corporation has set key objectives which are to:

- Strengthen the role of residents in influencing the design and delivery of services they receive
- Deliver high quality and cost-effective services
- Achieve continuous improvement in the services delivered to residents and others

A recent evaluation of the application of Best Value and tenant participation shows that many RSLs are applying the principles and actively involving tenants in the review process. A number have developed Tenant Participation Compacts or similar agreements, and more are planning to do so. A few are going further and are now looking to localise the approach through developing compacts across neighbourhoods or with particular groups of tenants, such as leaseholders, young people, or black and minority ethnic tenants.

For some RSLs this is familiar ground. There has always been a notable, albeit limited, tenant involvement strand within the housing association movement. Many RSLs have long seen their housing investment as part of a broader based approach to community regeneration, often referred to as Housing Plus. Relevant policies and initiatives include:

- **'Building on Success'** – part of the Corporation's Corporate strategy. It sets out how the Corporation will play its part in improving and revitalising deprived communities. The key aim is to invest in the creation of safe and sustainable communities by working in partnership to invest in sustainable new homes, and to develop new ways to enable housing associations and the Corporation to play an effective role in regeneration and neighbourhood renewal

- the Housing Corporation's **National Investment Strategy 2001/02** emphasised sustaining communities and a 'toolkit' is now part of the bidding process. All bids to the Approved Development Programme (ADP) have to relate the measures in the toolkit to the localities they wish to develop and to certify that they believe that the scheme will be sustainable

- **Innovation and Good Practice** (IGP) grants have encouraged RSLs to carry out action research projects testing out the practical measures they can take to support wider community regeneration

- **Community Training and Enabling** grants have been introduced to fill what is perceived as a gap in funding provision for RSL tenants – supporting initiatives aimed at involving residents in all aspects which impact on their homes

- the Housing Corporation's **tenant participation strategy** focuses on ways in which tenants might be collectively involved in consultation or participation processes

- meeting the needs of **black and minority ethnic communities** is a central feature of the Housing Corporation's overall strategy and guidance. The Housing Corporation has commissioned an independent evaluation of black and minority ethnic strategies within housing associations and has found that there is room for improvement. Its five year programme therefore aims to encourage a culture among RSLs that empowers black and minority ethnic communities and integrates their needs and aspirations into everyday business. The Corporation is also taking on board the recommendations of the 'Challenge Report' arising from the Race and Housing Inquiry for RSLs, external partners and the Corporation itself

- finally, as for local authorities, **modernising** has started to replace diversifying as the buzz word for structural and cultural changes to RSLs. The Housing Corporation has issued key consultation documents on modernising the governance of RSLs, *Modernising Governance: starting the debate*, *Modernising Governance: reporting the debate* and *Modernising Governance: an enabling approach*. The Chartered Institute of Housing in *Winning Structures* has argued for an alternative structure, a registered housing organisation, to enable RSLs to reshape their governance arrangements to combine effective service delivery with modern management and accountability

All of this fits well with the current Government policy on neighbourhood renewal, and Neighbourhood Management in particular.

CHAPTER 3

STRATEGIC WORKING

What this Chapter is about

This chapter considers the strategic framework within which
Neighbourhood Management fits including:

- The policy and practice of partnership working
- Finding appropriate funding for Neighbourhood Management
  initiatives
- How Neighbourhood Management fits in with the work of other sectors
- The challenges and tensions inherent in the Neighbourhood
  Management approach

A fundamental feature of Neighbourhood Management is the joined up
delivery of services. This requires a commitment to different departments and
agencies working together at every level of public policy making and service
delivery. Only in this way will services meet the real needs of residents and
achieve better and greater impact on the ground.

Service providers that have never worked together in a comprehensive way
will not only have to work closely with each other but also with the community
as an equal partner. Practical local strategies will have to identify the problems
and lead to the development of action plans which service providers,
communities and other stakeholders, such as the private sector, will need to
sign up to.

This is easier said than done. The historic and well-entrenched separation
between departments in large organisations, between agencies and between
programmes does not lend itself to integrated working. Each have their own
management and staffing structures, budgets and projects. Culturally, it could
be argued that their overall aim is to self-perpetuate, through increasing their
size, scale and scope, adapting to changing demands and priorities while
essentially sterilising anything that would force change or threaten established
customs and practices.

There is also an increasing range of agencies and special programmes responsible for delivering services in most areas – quite simply, there is more to join up. And it's not just the agencies which need to be working together, there are also businesses, voluntary organisations and community groups, as well as the most important ingredient, local people.

❑ Improving service delivery

The *Modernising Government* White Paper of March 1999 outlined a number of steps to improve access to public services, to ensure that people who may need services:

- Know what services are available
- Know how to apply for them
- Can easily do so:
  - preferably by a method that suits them best
  - at a time that suits them best
  - with help if they need it
  - with minimal delay

As a first step, the Effective Performance Division at the Cabinet Office has produced a checklist intended to help people at all levels in service delivery organisations to review access arrangements for the services they provide (see Appendix 6 for the website address). It provides a useful audit tool for an analysis of access to the services provided through Neighbourhood Management programmes.

❑ How can service providers work in partnership together?

The task of working together is enormous. Achieving joined up working in response to community needs is a major challenge. But it can, and must, be done. Perhaps more than any other of its component parts, Neighbourhood Management is dependent upon partnership working – partnerships will be the vehicles through which it is delivered.

In any Neighbourhood Management programme, there are likely to be four levels of partnership working:

- The Neighbourhood Management board at local level
- The other local initiatives across a wider area
- The city or district which may be the LSP
- The county or sub-regional level which may also be the LSP

Most housing organisations will already be involved in partnerships to a greater or lesser extent. They will be familiar with the potential benefits that can accrue. Unfortunately, they will also be familiar with the fact that any benefits are often in inverse proportion to the difficulties encountered. There is much practise of partnership working but too much of it is ineffective. In essence, there is little understanding of the things that make partnerships work in practical terms.

A partnership is essentially a practical structure to make things happen to the greater benefit of all beneficiaries and partners. For it to work, the following elements must be in place:

- Commitment and strong co-ordination at a strategic level between agencies
- Clarity about goals and the added value of a partnership
- Awareness about the contribution of each partner
- Time to build trust, respect and understanding
- Meaningful feedback into and from the partner organisations
- Follow up action outside meetings by partners
- Consistency and continuity of representation
- Leadership, and an open, inclusive culture
- Acceptance of the need for strengthening the skills and abilities of partners (capacity building)

Many partnerships, particularly at the local level, will also need an executive team. This ensures that action is implemented, that the partnership has its own identity and not the identity of one of the partners, that there is a spur to progress, and that the work of the partnership is monitored and reviewed.

Social landlords will be important partners in partnerships at all levels, but particularly at neighbourhood and local authority levels. At the local level, they are likely to be involved in partnerships which help them deliver their housing service in a more locally tailored and joined up way, and in many places this will mean Neighbourhood Management.

At this level, the likely factors for success in partnerships will be:

- Someone responsible at the neighbourhood level, such as a neighbourhood manager
- Community involvement
- Tools to get things done:
  - agreements with local service providers
  - devolved service delivery and purchasing
  - championing the neighbourhood
  - special resources
- A systematic, planned approach to problems
- Effective delivery mechanisms
- Commitment from service providers

At a sub-regional and city-wide level, social landlords with large stock holdings and/or a strategic role, who may already be focusing on special needs, young people or housing for elderly people, are also likely to be involved in partnerships. In a significant number of areas, these will be the new Local Strategic Partnerships.

Neighbourhood partnerships in Liverpool

Liverpool City Council has three aims in its approach to tackling neighbourhood renewal: improving housing and urban management; capacity building with communities and individuals, particularly to get them into jobs and training; and support for existing growth businesses and attracting inward investment.

A city-wide Local Strategic Partnership, the Liverpool Partnership Group has developed a 10 year strategic regeneration framework through its Liverpool First prospectus, which has clear cross-cutting themes and jointly agreed targets.

There are five strategic growth areas for business, including the City Centre, which have the same boundaries as the primary care trusts, area policing and target areas for European Union Objective 1 funding. The cluster partnerships are the intermediaries between the LSP and the neighbourhoods; they have their own boards with local business and community representation. A city-wide development company, in partnership with English Partnerships and the RDA, is the principal delivery vehicle for site assembly and marketing inward investment.

In each of the five cluster partnerships, all blue collar services will be under the supervision of one area manager. RSLs are zoned to take the lead for specific neighbourhoods and will develop relationships with them, which, at one end of the spectrum, may involve service level agreements and, at the other, holding area budgets themselves and overseeing procurement of services, effectively becoming the City Council's agent for service delivery.

❑ Partnership working in practice

Neighbourhood Management enables social landlords to work with a range of other agencies, service providers and organisations to improve services within a defined area. It allows for innovative ways of working, using new approaches, new powers and taking risks within a limited arena.

Clearly a much more strategic approach is necessary. The experience developed in working with a variety of other service providers on such multi-agency initiatives as community safety, neighbourhood watch, health action zones, one-stop shops, and out-of-school clubs will prove invaluable in Neighbourhood Management.

Linking health and housing, Castle Vale HAT

Castle Vale HAT was set up in 1993, following a tenant and leaseholder ballot, to regenerate Birmingham's largest post-war housing estate. It covers an area of 11,000 people.

The HAT inherited the task of turning round a problem that had been 30 years in the making. Health problems in particular were daunting; life expectancy was much lower than the regional average, infant mortality much higher than the regional average, incidences of drug and substance misuse, alcohol abuse, domestic violence, loan sharks and the stigmatism of a B35 post code signalled a neighbourhood suffering from disinvestment and lack of local services, apart from a health centre.

The HAT initiated baseline health studies early on. Partnerships were formed with health agencies and this was followed up by the development of multi-agency strategies which identified a range of much needed services. Over £2.5 million of health-related inward investment was attracted to Castle Vale as a result.

At the half way stage of the HAT's life, much work remains to be done but the benefits can be seen. Residents are now living longer. Fitter residents are gaining employment. Healthy babies are being given a better start in life; and residents can access locally provided services.

Some housing organisations have reorganised to make their delivery of services more local, more open and more responsive to the opinion of residents. These are key elements of working strategically.

Social Housing Agreement, Blackbird Leys, Oxford

At the Blackbird Leys estate in Oxford, a Social Housing Agreement between the City Council and local RSLs, led by Ealing Family HA, has committed them to a policy of community engagement and support, as well as ensuring that they all charge the same rents and take nominations from the Council. The agreement also ring-fenced rental income to prevent any leakage to other areas of the RSL's operation. Such agreements can provide the practical application of the strategic approaches developed by LSPs.

❑ From housing management to Neighbourhood Management

The delivery of housing services has been taking place at local level for some time. There are now many examples of the local delivery of housing services that can inform the development of Neighbourhood Management.

Local Service Delivery Plan, Manor Estate, Sheffield

North British Housing (NBH), part of the Places for People Group, started working on the Manor estate in Sheffield some 12 years ago. In the worst part, Vikinglea, 50% of the properties were empty, with many vandalised and burnt out. Yorkshire Metropolitan, South Yorkshire and Northern Counties Housing Associations also have housing on the estate. There are currently 1,000 new rented homes, a small element of shared ownership housing and 400 homes for sale being constructed by Bellways. Void property levels have now fallen to less than 2.5%. A local service delivery plan involves:

- A specialist Manor housing management team, with site services, located on the estate and delivering an intensive housing management service
- A Community Lettings Plan which recognised the fact that most lettings were to family and friends of existing residents whilst enabling decisive action against households which initiated anti-social behaviour
- NBH paying for additional police to increase foot and mobile patrols in the early stages
- Three estate caretakers to tidy up the estate, carry out minor repairs, clean and prepare voids for re-letting and liaising with estate managers about social problems and crime
- 15 estate officers, who are essentially manual staff carrying out minor repairs and maintenance and work across NBH's stock in Sheffield
- A Customer Contacts Officer, to keep close contact with people on the waiting list and support them in their new home, thus identifying people who would fit into the estate and those who would not
- A no boarding-up policy, instead using curtains to create a better impression, and to look attractive to potential tenants – properties are left empty until the right people are found for them
- Starter tenancies have been introduced to maintain the intensive management approach

A number of local authorities, RSLs and area-based programmes have long been involved in the tailoring and delivery of locally-based services. A recent Local Government Association (LGA) survey showed that out of 163 authorities which manage stock, 59% deliver housing management at neighbourhood level and 51% have or are planning to integrate these services with other local authority or public agency services.

The report from PAT 5 on Housing Management concluded that *'good housing management, with an on-the-spot presence, can make a real contribution to social exclusion by improving the quality of life for those in deprived areas'*. It advocates that local authorities and RSLs recognise the importance of good housing management and its contribution to neighbourhood renewal.

While strongly advocating the local delivery of housing services, the report from PAT 5 made the point very clearly that *'on its own, however, it (on-the-spot housing management) cannot eliminate social exclusion'*.

❏ The benefit of on-the-spot housing management

Lessons can, however, be learned from on-the-spot housing management, which shares many of the features of Neighbourhood Management:
- Customer-focused service delivery
- Resident involvement in service planning, delivery and monitoring
- Maximum access to service providers by service users
- Clear and speedy routes for redress for dissatisfied service users
- Service level agreements between providers and service users
- High calibre, well trained and remunerated housing managers
- Knowledge of/sensitivity to the area and its needs
- Strong racial and minority equality objectives
- Targeted use of new technology

Source: DETR (2001d)

The best models involve agreements, such as neighbourhood agreements being used at Foxwood in York and service level agreements being used at Burnley in Lancashire, to ensure clarity about the respective roles of tenants and housing managers.

It can be delivered through a variety of mechanisms:
- Estate based surgeries operated on a part-time basis, backed by a centrally based housing service

- Estate or neighbourhood-based offices giving a continuous presence during office hours
- Neighbourhood offices, or one-stop shops, with other departments and sectors
- Call centres operated centrally which give residents immediate access and aim to generate a quick response

Moving further towards the Neighbourhood Management model, some RSLs have tried joint management. On the Holly Street estate in the London Borough of Hackney, a consortium of five RSLs have established a joint management board involving residents. They have appointed an estate officer and three support staff, and developed a scheme of management to achieve common practice. The aim is to provide a unified service to all tenants.

On the Blackbird Leys estate in Oxford, three RSLs work from a shared on-site office and have developed a joint management agreement to harmonise standards, levels of service and methods of delivery.

Neighbourhood Initiative Teams, Threshold Tenant HA

Threshold Tenant Housing Association has established a Neighbourhood Initiatives Team, running two pilot schemes, including one promoting Neighbourhood Management in Earls Court, London, focusing on crime. The issues to be tackled include neighbour nuisance, security, drug dealing, and vulnerable young people. A series of public meetings led to a multi-agency forum headed by Notting Hill Housing Trust bringing together RSLs, the local authority, residents, local businesses, the voluntary sector and the police.

The RSLs and the local SRB programme funded a community development worker and began a programme of environmental and security improvements, and information technology training for residents. This has now become a partnership approach to developing Neighbourhood Management in the area, aimed at tackling:

- Neighbourhood Management and resident participation
- Allocations and reinvestment
- Caretaking
- Nuisance management
- Stock rationalisation and management
- Private sector improvement

❑ Finding the funding

Housing organisations that want to try Neighbourhood Management and have access to the funding to do so will either be involved in regeneration programmes or in receipt of dedicated funding. However, the majority will have to find creative ways of identifying funding through their own resources or, more likely, team up with providers of other services to pool funding and/or secure additional resources. (See Chapter 5).

❑ Potential funding opportunities

■ New Deal for Communities

This targets money available for deprived neighbourhoods to improve job prospects, bring together investment in buildings and in people and improve Neighbourhood Management and the delivery of local services. The 39 New Deal for Communities (NDC) areas are expected to implement Neighbourhood Management as part of their programmes and budgets. The local authority areas which receive funding from the Neighbourhood Renewal Fund – available for over three years to the 88 most deprived areas in England to help them and their partners begin to improve core public services – may also use the additional resources for Neighbourhood Management.

■ Neighbourhood Management pathfinder bids

A further 83 local authority areas (which contain more than one ward among the most deprived 10% in England, but excluding those where an NDC programme is already in place) were eligible to bid for pathfinder status with specific funding to implement Neighbourhood Management. The Government has initially made £45 million available for this programme over three years, with each pathfinder likely to receive an average of £500,000 a year. It is, however, expected that they will be financially supported for seven years. An initial group of 20 were selected from 72 bids in July 2001. A further group will be identified through a second round of bids.

It is expected that there will eventually be a national programme of 30 pathfinders (see Appendix 3). An additional four housing estates have been asked to participate as 'non-funded neighbourhood management pathfinder programmes'. These include Poplar Housing and Regeneration Community Association (HARCA) in Tower Hamlets, London; Royds Community Association in Bradford; Castle Vale Housing Action Trust in Birmingham; and Balsall Heath Forum in Birmingham.

Several SRB programmes are also experimenting with the approach.

A Housing Regeneration Company in Bradford

Bradford MBC and Bradford & Northern Housing Association are proposing to set up a housing regeneration company to assist with the delivery of neighbourhood renewal as part of SRB 6. This is in addition to the independent community-led company Regen 2000, which has been established to deliver the wider SRB 6 programme. The Housing Regeneration Company will contract with Regen 2000 to deliver the housing and environmental elements of the SRB strategy, which will include responsibility for partnership arrangements to deliver the social housing programme, private sector housing renewal and environmental improvements.

In addition, it will take responsibility for the development of local training and employment opportunities linked to these programmes. It will also be community-led, with local residents represented on its Board. Funding for the establishment of the new company is being provided by the SRB programme, through individual project proposals and staff secondments proposed from B&N and other private sector organisations. In the longer term, the aim is to establish a community-based organisation to deliver neighbourhood renewal and management and to develop a wider economic base.

❑ Funding for RSLs

RSLs have access to more limited sources of dedicated funding. These include:

- **Innovation and Good Practice (IGP) grants:** projects which support RSL involvement in Neighbourhood Management are likely to be a priority in the 2001/02 IGP strategy, and the Housing Corporation could, in principle, provide funding for pilots

- **Community Training and Enabling grants:** these are intended to pump-prime initiatives for residents to be effectively involved in decisions which affect their housing

On a more general level, the Housing Corporation's **Approved Development Programme (ADP)** may be skewed towards Neighbourhood Management projects, or, at least, community sustainability.

Several recent reports have argued for reallocating some of the current capital investment in bricks and mortar into revenue support for community sustainability, which would encompass Neighbourhood Management. This is particularly pertinent given the likely impact of the Government's rent restructuring proposals on the financial flexibility of RSLs to invest in neighbourhood renewal.

An idea from America which emerged from the Social Investment Task Force may provide access to funding for community investment generally for RSLs. It comprises:

- **A community investment tax credit (CITC)**, whereby investors in deprived areas would be entitled to a tax break that would be worth 25% of the value of their investment over five years. The Treasury could then offer an annual £50 million worth of tax concessions for five years (a community development venture capital fund or CDVCF), in order to attract a possible extra £1 billion of private sector money into the country's poorest areas

- **Community development financial initiatives (CDFIs)**, community banks that lend in deprived areas, which would bid for the right to offer the tax credit

- Successful CDFIs would become **community investment vehicles (CIVs)**, which could raise a specified amount of tax-advantaged investment

There may be opportunities here for RSLs, either individually, collectively or in partnership, to become a CDFI.

For many RSLs, the reality is that Neighbourhood Management will need to be accommodated within their current budgets. Some may be able to access other funding, for example by partnering with those local authorities which have access to dedicated money through the Neighbourhood Renewal Fund, New Deal for Communities programmes or as Neighbourhood Management pathfinders. There may be opportunities for RSLs to be the lead agent for Neighbourhood Management, or even Local Strategic Partnerships, nominated by the local authority and selected by the local community, which would act as the conduit for money. Some RSLs may consider subsidising Neighbourhood Management through rental income.

The majority of local authorities will not have access to special dedicated funding for Neighbourhood Management. They too will have to look at how to use existing resources creatively and to the maximum effect.

Neighbourhood Management in Balsall Heath, Birmingham

The Balsall Heath Forum in Birmingham operates in an area of 4,500 households. In 1996, it formed a Neighbourhood Strategic Partnership and obtained money from the URBAN European programme for four years.

Their long-term aim is to use existing money (from mainstream service budgets) in a better way via resident control rather than getting 'special' regeneration money, such as SRB or NDC. Where they have relatively easy access to special money, they use it to pave the way to getting mainstream funding. Consequently, their neighbourhood improvement programme is being funded and supported not by a large central budget but by a variety of partners making contributions through a variety of mechanisms:

- The police seconded a Chief Inspector to the area to pilot a neighbourhood manager role
- A local housing association, Prime Focus, subsequently seconded a neighbourhood manager for three days a week for two years
- A local housing association has handed over their landscaping budget to the Forum to apply and manage
- Five neighbourhood wardens are being funded through DTLR for two years with the aim of the long-term costs being picked up by partner agencies
- DTLR are also funding feasibility work around the development of a Tenant Management Organisation (TMO) to unify the management of the homes in the area (around 1,500 private rented and owned, around 1,500 in local authority ownership and around 1,500 in housing association ownership)

Extending this approach beyond their neighbourhood boundaries, the Forum believes that Balsall Heath will not become sustainable until the neighbourhoods around it are also renewed. Thus, it was instrumental in proposing that Birmingham's £11million of Neighbourhood Renewal Funds and £50million NDC funds should be applied across the city to include more than 30 neighbourhoods in a rolling programme of renewal (although this was not taken up).

Some would argue that this is exactly how it should be, that the amount of mainstream money going into deprived areas is more than enough to support the structures and mechanisms of Neighbourhood Management. Most would recognise, however, that the long-term under-investment in deprived neighbourhoods, particularly in the physical infrastructure, requires substantial special regeneration funding. Thereafter, the actual servicing of a Neighbourhood Management structure may not be prohibitively expensive and could, over time, actually reduce long-term public intervention. This has, of course, yet to be tested.

❏ Funding initiatives within or with other sectors

In keeping with the whole ethos of Neighbourhood Management, there are clear opportunities for housing organisations, both local authorities and RSLs, to team up with other sectors to pool budgets and identify additional funding. Neighbourhood Management will depend on a range of service providers from different sectors working together to meet shared objectives and deliver effective, sustainable change.

While there is a tension between these opportunities and the needs of service providers to achieve targets set by their own regulators, they will increasingly find that they cannot view their own indicators and targets in isolation. There will be a clear imperative to join forces to maximise resources.

Other key sectors have access to funding through a wide range of initiatives, many of them aimed at improving the lives of people living in deprived neighbourhoods (see Appendix 4 – Glossary of terms for details of funding initiatives).

■ Health

In the field of health, the NHS Plan signals a period of change in the provision of health care with a greater focus on tackling the health problems of people living in deprived urban communities. This will be implemented through initiatives such as Health Action Zones, Health Improvement Plans and personal medical services pilots. Primary Care Trusts are also now evolving into Care Trusts with the integration of National Health Service and local authority social services functions.

The new Supporting People programme requires that social landlords, health and social services providers work directly together to provide better support services for vulnerable people within the community. Therefore all sources of funding, including Housing Benefit currently paid to the provider (for instance RSLs) for the support of vulnerable people are integrated into a single, cash-limited fund which is then distributed at a local level by the local authority to the providers.

■ Education

In education, the drive to raise standards and individual attainment is being directed through existing programmes such as Sure Start, Education Action Zones and the Excellence in Cities programme. New initiatives include the Children's Fund, Connexions and the New Deal for Schools. In addition, there are related programmes for sport and culture, including Spaces for Sports and Arts for facilities in primary schools, Creative Partnerships which aim to ensure that every pupil in targeted deprived areas has access to cultural and creative opportunities and the existing Sports Action Zones.

■ Employment

Providing employment and training opportunities for all, particularly those in deprived communities, is perhaps the most important aspect of urban and rural renewal. Jobs bring money, confidence and purpose to an area. The poverty associated with large-scale unemployment is the greatest barrier to social inclusion. The link between housing and local employment has already been actively pursued by a number of local authorities and RSLs to provide employment and training in construction, maintenance, management and, latterly, through neighbourhood wardens.

Rebuild, Sheffield

Rebuild was a construction project set up, owned and run by a local voluntary board to act as both a training and construction vehicle in the Manor estate in Sheffield.

North British Housing (part of the Places for People Group) took the project on as a new build contractor. This gave the company confidence and capacity to develop and Rebuild has now successfully expanded into the fields of insulation and landscaping.

Rebuild now has a national reputation. It continues to work for the Association carrying out both new build, landscaping and rehabilitation contracts.

Current programmes should enable this link to be strengthened. The New Deal programmes, Employment Zones and Learning and Skills Councils, are being supplemented by Action Teams for Jobs, changes to benefits which encourage work accompanied by a more outward-looking role for the Benefits Agency, and positive action programmes to address racial discrimination through the New Deal Innovation Fund.

. . . .

Build and train, Penwith HA, Cornwall

Penwith Housing Association in Cornwall was formed in 1994 as a result of a stock transfer of some 3,600 homes from the local authority. One of its first Housing Plus initiatives was a Build and Train scheme to develop construction skills amongst local people. The trainees' 48 week programme consists of college-based and on-site training towards an NVQ qualification in their chosen trade. Trainees are paid a training allowance during the 48 week course and a variety of trades are offered.

While the trainees are not required to be tenants, the Association actively encourages applicants from its own stock through newsletters and open days. Trainees work with contractors across the association's development programme with a high proportion obtaining permanent work with the contractors with whom they have worked. 128 trainees have passed through the scheme to date and the programme now has European Social Fund support for 40 training places a year.

. . . .

Self build schemes and co-operatives are a further option. They are a group of people who come together in partnership with, for instance, RSLs, local authorities and local enterprise companies to improve their housing situation. The scheme offers training opportunities for unemployed people to build their own homes. Grants are available from the Housing Corporation and cover a variety of scheme types including rented accommodation, shared ownership and outright ownership.

■ Crime

The problems of crime and anti-social behaviour are familiar to all social landlords. It is an area in which they are becoming increasingly involved, given the relationship between crime, housing disrepair and abandonment, and neighbourhood decline. Anti-Social Behaviour Orders (ASBOs) offer one solution. RSLs have no statutory power to use ASBOs, although they may ask the local authority or the police to apply for an Order on their behalf. They will also need to work with local Crime and Disorder partnerships to develop strategies to reduce crime and disorder. In addition, RSLs should have strategies for identifying the extent of anti- social behaviour (including racial harassment) and for resourcing mechanisms to address the findings.

In this way police, local authorities, probation services and others are brought together to pool their efforts to fight crime.

Joint action against crime, South Yorkshire HA

The White City Estate in Maltby, South Yorkshire, was known as Little Beirut. It had a very poor reputation – vandalism, anti-social behaviour, arson, and drugs were rife on the estate of 250 homes. As part of a programme to refurbish the 157 housing association and local authority owned houses, South Yorkshire Housing Association provided a full-time senior housing management officer, a house as a focus for community involvement and activity and the establishment of a Community Partnership.

As well as the three landlords on the estate (SYHA, Rotherham Metropolitan Borough Council and a private landlord), this involves the police, the fire service, community groups and residents, and other statutory and voluntary agencies as and when needed. The initial focus was crime and disorder. Regular walkabouts with the police, landlords, environmental health officers and residents all helps to provide a visible show of unity and identify problems at an early stage. Joint landlord and police visits are undertaken where anti-social behaviour has both a civil and criminal element.

The police are committed to providing a higher profile presence in the area. This has led to an early drop in crime of more than 50%. This was followed by a joint statement by the three landlords to all residents making a strong commitment to dealing with anti-social behaviour, a local lettings policy, the involvement of the Community Partnership in the wider community beyond the estate, and the consolidation of stock with the private landlord swapping empty homes or selling to SYHA.

Today, the estate has negligible crime rates, greatly improved stock condition, a healthy waiting list, low turnover and an active Community Association.

Neighbourhood warden schemes are also being used to complement the work of the police and local authorities in agreed areas. There are also various programmes dealing with drug users and dealers. Some housing-led renewal schemes are paying for additional community police time, in response to resident demands for more visible policing. Poplar HARCA runs a 'Pay for Bobby' scheme along these lines.

■ Physical environment

A new Urban Bus Challenge scheme will be introduced to improve transport for deprived urban areas. The scheme will be based on the Rural Bus Challenge scheme which supports a hundred rural transport schemes. Home Zones which may include the provision of areas for children to play, environmental improvements or facilities, including places for parents to meet, may be established. Pilot schemes in England are currently being identified.

Further information on various plans and programmes can be found in Chapter 6 of the Urban White Paper, *Our towns and cities: the future, delivering an urban renaissance* (DETR, details in Appendix 6).

The lessons learned from the difficulties and rewards of working strategically are directly applicable. In particular, weaving together a number of funding streams from a variety of partners to establish a coherent, co-ordinated approach will require creative accountancy skills and the negotiating arts of a seasoned diplomat.

❑ Potential challenges and tensions

Neighbourhood Management will not be easy and some of the potential challenges and tensions are now considered.

■ Balancing service provision against the wider agenda

Finding the money to fund the local delivery of services tailored to the needs of local communities has been a challenge for housing organisations. There are conflicts between the pressure to keep rents low, to minimise Housing Benefit costs, encourage people into work, create mixed communities, and the need to invest in these communities to ensure that they are sustainable in the long term. See Finding the Funding above for discussion as to how this may be resolved

■ Community anxiety

All the research evidence suggests that local communities should be the real drivers for change in neighbourhoods. Some are already leading the renewal of their neighbourhoods and have been doing so for some time. Others are just embarking on the process. But for the majority of communities, taking a lead in their neighbourhoods is likely to be a completely new concept and one which may fill them with some trepidation.

For some, seeing a radical improvement in local services may be enough and they may not want to be directly involved, let alone take a lead role. Neighbourhood Management arrangements need to be flexible enough to accommodate different community perspectives and expectations. But for many communities, opening the door to a stronger say in their future will be a powerful force for change and one which will make a positive contribution to future neighbourhood sustainability.

■ Top down approaches

Some of the early Neighbourhood Management programmes have recognised the benefits it can bring to the need for a more strategic approach. As a result, they are tailoring some of the key modernisation mechanisms to assist in the delivery of Neighbourhood Management. In so doing, they are tackling the tension between the potentially top-down approaches of some of the elements of modernisation(such as local public service agreements) and the community-centred approach of Neighbourhood Management.

Public Service Agreement, East Brighton
New Deal for Communities

The East Brighton Community Partnership is implementing an NDC programme. They have produced a local public service agreement (PSA) to highlight targets that are critical to achieving their delivery plan outcomes and to gain agreement from local mainstream service providers on jointly achieving these shared targets. The agreement also contains standards for the way the East Brighton community and mainstream agencies will work together. It covers:

- Key outcomes and targets for the six themes in the NDC programme, education, health, employment, crime, environment and housing, and Neighbourhood Management
- Standards for working together (based on the city-wide compact)
- Joint undertakings of all partners, including specific undertakings of the community and undertakings on the statutory sector
- The process for implementation and review

There are eight service provider signatories to the PSA. It will be reviewed every six months. The specific details for delivering services and achieving targets in the PSA will be developed with individual agencies in the form of service level agreements.

Some housing organisations have reorganised to make their delivery of services more local, more open and more responsive to the opinions of residents. These are key elements of working strategically.

A growing number of local authorities are introducing 'area co-ordination' to integrate their services at a local level, often also bringing together other agencies, such as the police, health and education authorities. This approach also recognises that Neighbourhood Management is not a panacea for delivering local outcomes at the expense of broader policy making and service delivery across a wider area. Care has to be taken to ensure that residents are involved, the danger being that city/town wide structures could be top-heavy.

Local service delivery in Coventry

In Coventry, the local authority wanted to find an approach to the local delivery of services which could be implemented across the city and would involve all council services. This would enable economies of scale in terms of cost, equality of access to services and a strategic framework within which specific initiatives, such as Neighbourhood Management, could be tried out. There are six areas, each of which has a neighbourhood suffering problems of social exclusion, together with wealthier areas.

The key features which improve service delivery in Coventry are:

- Focusing the area divisions on the priority neighbourhoods, that is, those most in need of support and improvement
- Common boundaries where possible with other service providers, such as the local Primary Care Trust and the Education Action Zone
- Each area having dedicated staff – a co-ordinator, community development worker, community safety workers, and client agency staff (to develop Best Value street services)
- Aiming to recruit new staff from communities within the areas
- Each area having a multi-disciplinary team comprised of officers from council service departments, other service agencies and community representatives
- Each area team having a budget for community initiatives and capacity building work
- All areas producing an area plan, detailing actions to develop, improve and co-ordinate services, and to bid for funding
- The area system leading on social exclusion and improving the delivery of services, supporting the council's modernisation agenda
- Linking the area staff into the management structure across departments and to a senior level
- Action groups of residents, community groups and front-line staff in each area focusing on locally relevant issues
- A close link to the LSP for the city, the Strategic Partnership Group
- Each area having a public forum led by ward councillors, a member of the Cabinet, area staff and a senior director

■ Making it happen

There are tremendous challenges in bringing together all the partners who need to be involved in LSPs. A range of approaches will be needed to bring relevant partners on board in the first place, keep them there and encourage them to play an active role. Partners will want to see a strategic, dynamic forum which they feel is doing rather than talking. Many institutional partners need to be encouraged out of a mentality of partnership fatigue and cynicism by a new sense of direction and purpose.

Involving local communities will be critical to the success of LSPs. But there are clear tensions between thinking strategically and acting locally. Balancing the power between neighbourhoods and the centre will necessitate thoughtful structuring and management of the LSP. Care will need to be taken to ensure that local communities are represented and have the potential to play a leading role.

For instance, funds such as the Community Empowerment Fund (see Appendix 2) can be used to promote and support community involvement and decisions on its use should involve communities themselves.The relationship between an LSP and the local authority will also require careful consideration. Whilst they are probably best placed to bring potential partners together, it may be that another partner should lead the LSP.

The role of regional government offices is significant. They will act as facilitators to support the development of LSPs, as mediators in resolving any difficulties, and as accreditors to monitor grant conditions and genuine community participation. Clearly, the application of these roles will be important to the success of an LSP. Moreover, they will not only have to identify infringements or poor practice, but also take remedial action. This may require a much more assertive approach than some regional government offices will be used to.

There are three further areas which will be important elements of successful Neighbourhood Management; the role of councillors and RSL board members; the potential for Neighbourhood Management in rural areas and the inclusion of the private sector.

■ A new role for councillors and RSL board members

The change of approach required to make Neighbourhood Management work demands changes of everyone involved, not the least of these being the emphasis on community involvement and leadership. The Local Government Act 2000 specifically requires elected backbench members to:

- Become 'champions of their community'
- 'Spend less time in council meetings and more time in the local community'
- Reflect local people's concerns and priorities rather than 'defending council decisions'

These new requirements are being further extended by the implications of stock transfers. Historically, councillors have had a key role in housing, but with the increasing transfer of housing stock away from local authorities to other landlords, this role will change dramatically. Conversely, the transfer of much of this stock to RSLs will enhance the role of RSL board members. The new interface between the two will require a complete re-appraisal of roles and relationships.

In traditional RSLs, the primary obligation of board members is to the company and they have consequent legal responsibilities. In new style local housing companies, the board is likely to be composed of both independent board members, councillors and elected tenant representatives. Again, their primary duty is towards the company.

For Neighbourhood Management to work, many councillors will need to change the way they think and operate. They will need to prioritise representing the interests of local people, rather than the interests of their political parties or the local authority. They will need to be supported to do so, both through the policies and structures of the local authority and through specific training, information and access to up to date communication services.

A checklist of the actions required to develop a more representational role for councillors could equally be a checklist for effective representation in Neighbourhood Management:

- Review the support councillors need to be effective representatives
- Ensure that the organisation's complaints system is used to monitor performance
- Review communications systems to and from localities
- Reform the committee system to reflect the representational role
- Consider how the council can best consult and involve people involved in each ward
- Consider how the representative role will link into the executive decision-making role

Source: Filkin, G (2000)

A combination of change and clarity is going to be essential to a successful re-working of the role of councillors, and RSL board members, generally and in their involvement in Neighbourhood Management. Successful Neighbourhood Management programmes are likely to be independent of local authorities, whilst requiring their close involvement, and will often be led by RSLs as the main landlord.

In specific terms, the role of councillors in Neighbourhood Management is two-fold. First, to represent constituents individually and collectively in pursuit of their concerns, interests and rights. Second, where applicable, to represent the landlord. In practical terms, this could include:

- Acting as local champions within the neighbourhood
- Acting as a champion of the neighbourhood with the local authority and partner organisations
- Being a member of a Neighbourhood Management board/partnership
- Providing a link between neighbourhood initiatives, area-wide development and town/city strategies
- Monitoring and influencing the delivery of services through membership of Overview and Scrutiny Committees in local authorities

Source: Abstracted from LGA (2001)

It will be in the interests of councillors to see Neighbourhood Management as an opportunity to re-define and re-focus their role in the wake of the structural changes caused by modernisation. While the modernisation process potentially improves the efficacy of strategic planning and service delivery it has left the majority of councillors struggling with the scrutiny system outside the power base of the new cabinets.

Neighbourhood Management provides councillors with a new role, which has the potential to remove the burdens of conflict between party loyalty and the desires of local communities. Instead, it offers the opportunity to really speak and act for the neighbourhood, to focus their attention on local issues, and create a new role which achieves the very thing councillors say they want but are often prevented from doing – effectively and unambiguously representing local people.

■ **Neighbourhood Management – the rural dimension**

The potential for Neighbourhood Management in rural areas presents a second significant challenge. There is a tendency to think that Neighbourhood Management is a solution to urban problems. But while it will be tried and tested predominantly in urban communities, there is a clear rural dimension.

Around 16 of the 88 areas receiving Neighbourhood Renewal Fund money have significant rural aspects.

The Rural White Paper provides the overall context within which rural regeneration will take place and within its 10 targets includes four which specifically apply to housing and the local delivery and improvement of services:

- Support for village services, using rate relief, renewing the Post Office network and creating a community service fund
- Modernising rural services, improving health services, providing internet learning and access points, and increasing resources for rural policing
- Providing affordable homes, by developing more homes through Housing Corporation funding, better use of the planning system in respect of private developments, and potentially charging full council tax on second homes
- Giving local power to country towns and villages, developing community plans, supporting quality town and parish councils, and developing a rural information technology network

Community Regeneration Zones in Blackburn with Darwen

Blackburn with Darwen Borough Council has established a network of community regeneration zones (CRZ), including one in a rural area. They are intended to address the same issues of service improvement and innovation, partnership working, a joined up approach, community participation and social exclusion as Neighbourhood Management. Each CRZ has developed a local strategy and action plan, linked to the Borough-wide community plan. In addition, it is linked to the public service agreement negotiated with the Government, a key target of which is the reduction of rural poverty and isolation in the East Rural Ward.

A number of community development officers in Blackburn with Darwen will act as neighbourhood managers to:

- Research further the issues faced by local people living and working in the ward
- Co-ordinate targeted action to address these issues through a Community regeneration board
- Attract additional resources for local projects, such as improved access to services
- Work closely with existing structures and partnerships, such as the parish council

The success of approaches to Neighbourhood Management in rural areas, which may be better referred to as village or town management, will depend upon a clear understanding of the issues and, specifically, how they will differ from those that arise in urban areas:

- An imaginative approach towards obtaining resources (government programmes being mainly focused on high density urban neighbourhoods)
- Tailoring capacity building and resident involvement approaches to take account of distance, isolation, differences, and unfamiliarity with community involvement
- Acknowledging the net migration of services from rural areas over the last 20 years, leaving isolated, unsupported communities
- Making the case for funding when areas of affluence and/or close deprived urban areas can distort the picture and/or dominate the competition for resources
- Recognising that the partners will be different and maybe unused to working in partnership
- Understanding that community facilities are limited, and village halls can be inaccessible, thus making it difficult to focus activity

There are already approaches being tried that could start the process of village or town management:

- Village design statements, to inform planning guidance with the views of residents
- Village appraisals, to identify the weaknesses and strengths of an area to inform regeneration plans
- Village companies, to provide a comprehensive approach to rural problems
- Community regeneration zones, to facilitate change in areas of rural decline

A number of RSLs and local authorities are developing models which are beginning to translate Neighbourhood Management into a rural environment. These are important projects which need to be widely replicated.

Village companies in Nottinghamshire

LHA (formerly Leicester Housing Association) has developed a village company at Whaley Thornes and Langwith, a relatively isolated, largely rural area of dispersed villages and small towns near Mansfield dramatically affected by pit closures. The company is an Industrial and Provident Society and its overall aim is to contribute to the rebuilding of vibrant and thriving communities by attracting funding, stimulating enterprise and employment initiatives, and raising capital.

The company can trade as a business, employ staff and construct and deal in property. The elected board has nine members, three from the local District Council, three local residents and three stakeholder representatives. It also acts as a parent company for three wholly owned subsidiary trading businesses providing property services, decorating services and gardening services, which provide training and employment for local people. One of its current projects is the acquisition of a small number of shops to be let to the local community for commercial business use – a fish and chip shop opened recently and will be followed by a butchers and a post office.

Planned projects include:

- A community resource centre and office base for the company
- 40 new mixed tenure homes
- Refurbished allotments
- Improved street lighting
- A relocated play area
- A new nature area on currently derelict land

The funding has come from the Coalfield Task Force, Bolsover District Council, the Housing Corporation, SRB 6 and the East Midlands Development Agency.

■ Working with the private sector

Many regeneration schemes have tried to attract funding or support from business. Most have failed to achieve the levels hoped for. Increased opportunity for business to participate has not resulted in significant involvement. Where it has, residents have not always been convinced that they add value or deliver better services.

There is an argument that Government needs to adopt tougher tactics, including legislation, if it wants to create a socially and environmentally responsible business culture. Current proposals include:

- Greater co-ordination across Government through the regional co-ordination unit bringing together social and economic initiatives
- The New Deal for Employment programme having a much greater engagement by employers
- Business improvement districts to give businesses the lead in shaping and delivering regeneration of inner-city areas

- Fiscal changes and funding instruments to deliver regeneration, such as the CDFI and gearing tax liabilities to the degree to which a range of environmental and social costs are already paid for by a company

Source: Griffiths, J (2001)

....

Private sector involvement
Castle Vale Housing Action Trust, Birmingham

In 1993, Castle Vale had an unemployment rate of 26% and the area experienced postcode stigmatisation. A local business group was established with six members. Its aim was to bring together local employers, establish their future plans and staff requirements and initiate training programmes tailored to meet them. By 2001 the group had grown to more than 60 members and unemployment had been reduced to 5.8%, below the Birmingham average.

The private sector is also an important investor in Castle Vale. While the Housing Action Trust has been well funded by Central Government, additional funding was needed to achieve the changes necessary to regenerate the area. To date, it has levered in £72 million of private and other funding. This has been achieved through commercial, residential, industrial and recreational developments. In addition, the private sector has played an important part in improving the image of Castle Vale.

....

Initiatives have to be taken at the local level also. Neighbourhood Management programmes will have to find ways of involving business. The three most likely levels of involvement are:

- **As a partner**, represented at management/board level or as a stakeholder supporter of the programme
- **As a delivery agent**, maybe as part of a business grouping which could access small sums of money to put together a neighbourhood strategy and lead the process. In reality, the delivery role is more likely to come about through the contracting out of services resulting from Best Value, with the local authority retaining the strategic approach and the private sector having a role in the implementation
- **As local landlords**, in inner city areas, where large numbers of properties may be owned by private landlords. Some of these will be companies specialising in acquiring low value housing for rent, mainly to benefit claimants; others will be individuals with one or two houses acquired as an investment. There is also a trend in low demand areas of homeowners letting out homes which, due to negative equity, they are unable to sell

Where landlords are organised through a Private Owners Forum or Association, there may be opportunities for negotiating successful partnering arrangements, stock rationalisation and service agreements. Carrots and sticks are both likely to be required. Managing neighbourhoods where private landlords are active without involving them is unlikely to be successful. They will want to know exactly what the benefits of involvement and support will be. They will need to be able to see tangible benefits. There are a limited number of ideas here:

- Offering specific and measurable incentives, such as improved street cleaning or better security, for which they would contribute
- Requesting an annual fee against which there would be guaranteed improvements to the area which would decrease their costs, such as reducing crime which would, in turn, lower their insurance premiums
- Using the successful approaches adopted for town centre management

The relationship between the state and business has begun to change and government is actively seeking attractive new ways to increase the role business can play. One of the tests for Neighbourhood Management programmes will be the extent to which they can persuade, cajole and attract business to become involved whilst at the same time making use of new measures at Government level and innovative incentives at the local level.

❑ What do service providers in general, and housing providers in particular need to do to make sure strategic/partnership working actually works?

The New Deal for Communities initiative is one of the first concerted efforts by Government to invest substantial neighbourhood renewal resources in communities themselves. Working in partnership with local authorities, registered social landlords and others, they are expected to take the lead in developing delivery plans and managing the programmes. It is a challenging and dynamic process which requires a significant investment in community capacity building and development, much of it at the front end of the process. It will take time to deliver successfully, particularly in those communities starting from a low 'empowerment base'.

Successful Neighbourhood Management poses a similar challenge for professionals. But it would be misleading to think that the process of engaging with communities is limited to running training and support programmes and employing a few community development workers. Fundamentally, it is about shifting the balance of power in neighbourhoods towards residents and, by implication, away from professionals and their agencies. Creating and sustaining genuinely community-led partnerships, with the traditional roles between professionals and residents reversed, is likely to be one of the keys to sustainable Neighbourhood Management.

This is a challenging notion for professionals and their organisations and one which may be seen by some as threatening. It need not be. Beginning the process of putting it into practice is likely to involve a range of measures in each neighbourhood.

Measures to change the balance of power in neighbourhoods

- **Written contracts or concords** between neighbourhood communities and agencies involved in local partnerships

- **Community majorities on, and chairs of, elected neighbourhood boards** set up to deliver Neighbourhood Management

- Support for existing and potential **community entrepreneurs or champions**, to strengthen community leadership in neighbourhoods

- **Community-led consultation** with the wider community, using a variety of 'what works' techniques

- **Locally-determined capacity building** measures, to broaden the base of community involvement

- **Community representatives providing training for professionals**, particularly those with direct responsibility for neighbourhood services

- **Networking** with other Neighbourhood Management initiatives

- **Locating local authority staff and agency professionals in neighbourhoods**, working from community owned or managed neighbourhood centres

---

Neighbourhood Management initiatives need to work with the grain of local politics. Local authorities need to step back, take a more strategic approach to neighbourhood renewal and share power with local communities at neighbourhood level. Doing so successfully is as much about trusting community leaders as anything else. In the past, community leaders have often been regarded as mavericks. There has been a tendency for local authorities and others to work closely with community leaders they feel they can influence and less closely with those they feel they cannot.

Local authorities and RSLs often place considerable weight on the formal recognition of representative structures and much less on working with people who have the confidence of their community and can drive change. The results can be counter-productive. Neighbourhood Management will not work on this basis; representative structures are important, but they need to be inclusive and democratic. Sharing power in principle, but not in practice will quickly be seen by local communities as a facade and may inevitably lead to conflict and division.

In conclusion, the wider agenda around modernisation is essentially about change. Whilst ostensibly a small part of modernisation, the principles of Neighbourhood Management share many of the features of the modernising programme. The key issues in modernisation are the same as those which will apply at a local level in determining the success or failure of Neighbourhood Management:

- Social landlords examining the relationship between themselves and their communities
- The need to remove organisational and departmental boundaries
- The breaking down of departmental/service budgets
- Trying different approaches to involving the community and developing its strength
- Improved communication at all levels
- Improved service delivery through corporate and partnership working
- Self-reliant front-line staff
- New roles for councillors, RSL board members, and community organisations
- Flexible ways of working
- A commitment to open decision making

Source: Abstracted from Burgess, Hall, et al, JRF (2001)

Both are essentially about improving services, finding new ways of identifying and meeting local priorities; and involving local communities and residents in decision making and implementation. As such, Neighbourhood Management can greatly assist social landlords in delivering the wider modernisation agenda.

CHAPTER 4

INVOLVING THE COMMUNITY

What this Chapter is about

This chapter deals with the key role local communities must play in
Neighbourhood Management and sets out how housing organisations can
help facilitate it, including:

- Community development and capacity building

- Community consultation and involvement

- Engaging with black and minority ethnic communities

- Working with rural communities

- Empowering communities and community leadership

- Funding community involvement

*'Neighbourhood Management...could provide a way of genuinely empowering
deprived communities. Instead of just giving communities some influence over a
transitory pot of special money, it would give them long term leverage over the main
services that affect the lives of those who live there.'*

Source: SEU (2000a)

The involvement of local communities in Neighbourhood Management will
undoubtedly be the key to its success. As Chapter 3 pointed out, shifting the
balance of power in neighbourhoods from service providers to residents is the
key to sustainability and, therefore, also to the long-term success of the
Neighbourhood Management idea. It will not be easily achieved. Fortunately
there is plenty of good practice around. Communities have been heavily
involved in renewal programmes for some time, but few have managed to
establish genuine power-sharing arrangements with service providers and only
a handful have taken the lead.

This chapter provides some guidance on what needs to be put in place to give local communities a central role in the Neighbourhood Management process.

❑ Community development

Changing the balance of power in neighbourhoods depends, in part, on providing local communities and individuals with the *support* they need to engage with professionals and their agencies on an equal basis (community development).

Community development is likely to be a critical aspect of successful Neighbourhood Management and one which needs to be adequately resourced. Up to now, local authorities have been the main employers of community development workers, but their numbers have been dwindling in recent years. Many areas being targeted for Neighbourhood Management have little or no community development support.

Many registered social landlords have now established community development teams and this is encouraging; other agencies involved in neighbourhood service delivery will need to do the same. They can provide a clear mechanism through which local communities can engage with agencies normally seen as remote and inaccessible.

Strengthening the ability of local groups to build their structures, systems, people and skills, often referred to as capacity building, is an essential part of a broader community development approach. It is the starting point for achieving sustainable change in neighbourhoods.

Work to increase the understanding and influence of communities in Neighbourhood Management needs to be closely tailored to local circumstances – flexibility is the key. Wherever possible, the type of capacity building needed in a neighbourhood should be defined and agreed by the community itself. It is vital to work at the community's pace.

Capacity building approaches

- Agree a capacity building plan
- Set priorities and budgets for the plan
- Secure the necessary funding
- Start with building confidence in individuals

- Run regular training sessions for community representatives
- Hold residential and community-based courses
- Provide mentoring and shadowing for individuals
- Offer personal development programmes
- Provide community leadership programmes
- Make links to other forms of personal and group learning
- Offer organisational development support and advice
- Access support and advice from appropriate specialist agencies
- Specifically target excluded groups; i.e. young people, black and minority ethnic groups and people with disabilities.

Many professionals are likely to assume that residents require intensive training before they can be expected to participate in decisions about Neighbourhood Management. This is not always so – most people learn best 'on the job' and formal training sessions, however well delivered, can put people off.

Capacity building is a high risk activity; the outcomes are never known in advance; the local people involved are almost always under pressure, personally, socially and economically. Community representatives are volunteers; many of them are involved in a wide range of activities and local organisations. Living where they do exposes them to the everyday pressures of life in deprived neighbourhoods. Many suffer from poor health, partly from the stress and long hours they put in.

Perhaps not surprisingly, consultation fatigue and burn out are increasingly common. As community involvement in neighbourhood renewal generally becomes ever more important, so this particular issue is likely to rise up the agenda.

Neighbourhood Management plans therefore need to:
- Work within the capacity of individuals
- Plan for a potential turnover of key individuals
- Examine ways of offering volunteers payment for their work if appropriate
- Broaden the base of community activity to enable workloads to be shared
- Ensure that those involved have real influence and can see early results

Delivering capacity building to local communities involves resources and needs dedicated staff. These staff may well be employed initially by the lead agency for Neighbourhood Management, but they should ideally be seconded to work directly for a community-led neighbourhood board. Their role will encompass some or all of the capacity building approaches set out above. In Balsall Heath, Birmingham, capacity builders are at the centre of the Neighbourhood Forum's self help approach to Neighbourhood Management and renewal.

Capacity building staff functions in Balsall Heath

- Meeting the training requirements of 20 residents and other groups
- Identifying and supporting 60 plus 'good neighbours'
- Enabling local groups to access resources and realise their vision
- Supporting residents involved in championing the Neighbourhood Plan
- Enabling young people to play a part in renewal
- Enabling residents to develop their own diverse interests and build one strong community
- To help wire-up the community with IT skills and equipment, so that everyone can communicate with everyone else
- To enable residents to earn income by managing social enterprises
- To enable residents to lead the management of their own neighbourhood
- To set up an academy for renewal

Source: Balsall Health Forum (2001b)

Building community capacity through Neighbourhood Management can also create local jobs and support local economies. New neighbourhood services can be provided by residents themselves, whilst existing ones can target local people for recruitment. Some RSLs, particularly members of People for Action 2001 Limited, a membership organisation for regeneration and housing organisations, have a long history of generating local employment through their community investment activities. Much of this has, in the past, been focused around construction and development, but Neighbourhood Management opens up new opportunities for service jobs (for instance caretaking and neighbourhood wardens) of a less transitory nature.

Resident's concerns about community safety and anti-social behaviour can also be used to help build capacity and generate local employment.

Neighbourhood wardens in East Brighton

The East Brighton New Deal for Communities Team turned to Chichester Diocesan Housing Association, part of the Hyde Group, rather than the local authority, to be the lead agent in providing services. It wanted to bring in new ideas and approaches to address residents' criticisms of existing public services.

One of the first initiatives has been the introduction of neighbourhood wardens as on-site customer service staff. The neighbourhood warden service is designed to employ and train local people to provide a service for the benefit of their local community. The wardens are not intended to provide an alternative policing service, but to work closely with police and other agencies to deal with issues of anti-social behaviour, and harassment.

The wardens are also very much involved in welcoming new residents to the area and ensuring that they settle into their new homes, and ensuring that problems associated with rubbish dumping, street lighting, graffiti and other environmental problems are dealt with speedily. They are also intended to support the work of resident and community groups and to provide a good neighbour support to any resident who wishes to use their services.

However, initiatives aimed at employing local residents through Neighbourhood Management need to be carefully targeted, with appropriate support provided for individuals. Sustainable jobs are not always achievable, not least because some residents may find it difficult to cope with the pressures of 'living on the job'.

Estate caretakers at Blackbird Leys, Oxford

Initially, Ealing Family HA and Oxford Citizens HA employed a community caretaker as part of their work on the Blackbird Leys estate in Oxford. The caretaker provided a range of local services, including cleaning, litter picking, some minor repairs and looking after three community centres. Originally they were required to be residential on the estate, but the pressures of 'living on the job' resulted in a high turnover of staff.

More recently, Ealing Family HA decided to recruit a non-residential handyperson who will be more involved in helping residents to carry out a wide range of minor repairs, and a non-residential caretaker concentrating on the community centres (although, in the event, both live nearby). This was agreed after consultation with residents, who particularly asked for a handyperson.

❏ Consultation and involvement

Housing providers and managers, amongst others, have been involved in consultation with residents for many years, particularly about new developments, housing management, and rent setting; it is certainly not a new thing. The days when tenant participation was seen as an optional extra by providers of social housing are long gone. A wide variety of techniques and approaches are now being used. There is an extensive national network of tenants' and residents' associations, forums and federations, supported by an array of professional trainers and service agencies.

The introduction of Best Value and Tenant Participation Compacts in 2000, initially through local authorities and increasingly through registered social landlords, has begun to radically increase the involvement of tenants in the delivery of housing services and particularly in the management of their homes. But the vast majority of compacts negotiated so far are council-wide; there are few neighbourhood compacts and this is likely to represent an important element in the development of future Best Value arrangements.

Many new registered social landlords have been formed through the stock transfer process, with tenants centrally involved in the process, supported by tenant's friends through to the ballot stage and having often substantial representation on each new Board. Social housing landlords have had to learn many new consultation tricks to bring people on board at an early stage and keep them there throughout a long and highly complex process.

The introduction of Neighbourhood Management needs to build on these existing techniques and mechanisms, working wherever possible with well-established consultation arrangements and not automatically introducing new structures. However, in many neighbourhoods, these arrangements may require better co-ordination or they may just need refreshing – some long-established residents' associations may be just ticking over, or no longer representative. Housing professionals therefore need to constantly encourage and support residents' associations in their efforts to engage new people and be accountable.

To be successful and sustainable, Neighbourhood Management needs to be inclusive. It needs to draw in all the representative community organisations in a neighbourhood, possibly through the creation of a neighbourhood forum – an umbrella body with a specific neighbourhood focus.

The key elements of a successful community consultation and involvement approach to Neighbourhood Management and renewal are likely to include:
- Getting local people involved right from the start
- Using 'what works' methods of disseminating information – it will be different in each community

- Prioritising informal and participative methods of consultation – avoiding formal public meetings
- Targeting hard to reach groups, particularly those that do not normally get involved in community activities.
- Helping to put new structures in place where no suitable neighbourhood ones exist
- Recruiting local people onto these new structures and encouraging ownership of the process
- Encouraging flexibility, so that these structures can evolve as residents gain in confidence and experience
- Developing residents' leadership skills
- Promoting and sustaining democratic neighbourhood representation through annual elections
- Running an extensive community consultation process using well-established techniques (community planning; planning for real; citizens' juries; ballots)
- Developing neighbourhood or community plans which outline residents' agendas for change
- Providing community development and capacity building support and, when needed, independent advice
- Creating a culture of trust, transparency and accountability, with no hidden agendas
- Treating residents as equals and working with them on this basis
- Training and supporting community representatives involved in Neighbourhood Management delivery
- Providing community access to resources to pursue their own objectives
- Moving at the community's pace, allowing adequate time for consultation and involvement to be effective
- Being process-led, not funding-led
- Focusing on good communications, providing maximum, rather than minimum information to residents

Community involvement in Waltham Forest Housing Action Trust

The Waltham Forest HAT owns four large housing estates in the London Borough of Waltham Forest. It began its work in 1992. In each area tenants elected an Estate Steering Group on an annual basis and these tenants once elected represented their area in discussions and negotiations with the HAT and other agencies.

The Estate Steering Group developed over time and in the mid-90s became very powerful and influential with the remit to call HAT officers to their meeting and the ability to comment on any report on the agenda on the HAT Board. Over time these groups have transformed into Local Committees which have a similar level of involvement.

The Local Committees have a significant influence in decisions made by the HAT and the Community Based Housing Association within their own area. The HAT Board meetings now rotate around each of the four areas and the Local Committee in the area where the meeting is to be held have a right to put any items on the Board agenda and to make representations at the Board meeting. The Local Committees are consulted in advance to identify any issues they wish to raise and if appropriate a HAT officer writes a report for that agenda item which is circulated to Board Members prior to the meeting. In this way HAT Board Members and HAT officers are accountable to local residents and decision making is more transparent.

On each of the four estates there are four-weekly meetings involving representatives of the main HAT contractors/consultants and these are known as Corporate Estate Teams (CETs). Tenant representatives are invited to all CET meetings and at least one tenant, sometime two or three, attend. They can participate in the meeting on the same basis as any of the participants and this is an effective way of identifying any problems or issues that are still outstanding and sharing information.

❑ Kick-starting the process

The way service providers engage with communities needs to be tailored closely to local circumstances. All the techniques need to be used on a 'what works' basis. Some tried and tested methods of kick-starting the process, many of them identified in the Policy Action Team 4 report, include:

- Setting up a **community forum** to bring residents together, start discussing neighbourhood agendas and begin to develop an action plan
- Establishing a **neighbourhood board**, with elected resident representatives and service providers working together to tackle neighbourhood problems
- **Engaging with non-participants**, through questionnaire surveys, ballots and call centres, using IT facilities and other innovative techniques to spread the engagement to people who rarely have a voice; eg young people; those whose first language is not English, those who lack basic reading and writing skills; or those that do not have a phone

- **'Quick win' projects** which create local employment or open up new opportunities for volunteering. Neighbourhood wardening, caretaking, cleaning, recycling, maintenance of open spaces and minor repairs can all be done by local people and could make a vital contribution to the success of Neighbourhood Management and demonstrate to sceptical residents that things are changing
- Finding **local social entrepreneurs**, able to lead a community through the early stages of Neighbourhood Management, perhaps working with other individuals who have developed their own project ideas and received funding support
- Using innovative **community planning or visioning** techniques, to reach large numbers of people
- Using **local intermediaries**, particularly those with a stake in the neighbourhood, to pump-prime the community involvement process. These could be anything from registered social landlords, through councils for voluntary service, to micro-social enterprises – small, informal organisations or networks working 'unseen' in many neighbourhoods
- Setting up a network of **street-based groups**, to build a community forum or neighbourhood board from the bottom up

Whatever the mechanism or structure, the checklist below outlines a process, or sequence of events, which could be used to get communities involved in discussions about how Neighbourhood Management should be delivered.

A checklist for involving local communities in Neighbourhood Management

✔ Raise awareness about who is responsible for the delivery of neighbourhood services

✔ Explain how neighbourhood services are funded, who holds the budgets and the mechanism for agreeing them

✔ Keep residents informed about any proposed changes in delivery arrangements

✔ Discuss community needs and expectations of local services, using 'what works' techniques; i.e. those tailored to local circumstances

✔ Agree community priorities for future service delivery

✔ Decide on the type of services residents want to influence

✔ Decide on any services residents want to deliver themselves

✔ Agree standards residents wish these services to achieve

✔ Regularly monitor service delivery performance

✔ Promote the delivery of new neighbourhood services

Delivering everything on this checklist will not be easy; it will take time and energy from everyone involved to achieve them.

❏ Engaging with black and minority ethnic communities

Taking concerted action to consult with and involve black and minority ethnic communities in regeneration has, until recently, been the preserve of a minority of social landlords. It has tended to be a priority for black-led RSLs, local authorities and RSLs working with significant black and minority ethnic communities, and in the few places where pressure from black and minority ethnic communities themselves has persuaded, or forced, social landlords to act.

Given the overwhelmingly white culture of the great majority of housing organisations, this is perhaps not surprising. What is surprising is the gap between the seemingly widespread acceptance of the need to take measures to consult with and involve black and minority ethnic communities and actually doing it.

'Getting engaged' in Lambeth

Presentation Housing Association is one of the largest black and minority ethnic RSLs with over 4,000 homes across 23 local authorities. It has recently embarked upon a three year project called 'Getting Engaged' funded by the Housing Corporation's IGP grant programme and in partnership with the London Borough of Lambeth. The aim is to identify the practical, social and cultural barriers to black and minority ethnic involvement in regeneration. The key features are:

- A focus on a discrete geographical area in Lambeth undergoing stock transfer and renewal
- It will pilot new ways of consulting and involving black and minority ethnic communities
- It will link consultation and involvement with practical outcomes, i.e. physical development
- It will prioritise outreach work as a method
- It will innovate and take risks, trying out a range of methods and ideas
- Publicising the findings

The findings will be publicised and disseminated to a wide range of housing organisations that wish to develop their work with black and minority ethnic communities.

The experience of those social landlords who have been successful in involving black and minority ethnic communities suggests that there is no great mystery to it. The principles for consulting with and involving black and minority ethnic communities are broadly the same as those for any community:

- Tapping into their (not always overtly expressed) desire to be actively involved, instead of treating them as passive recipients
- Understanding that they may want to be involved at every level, including management and delivery
- Ensuring that consultation and involvement leads to action which reflects the views and needs expressed
- Ensuring they are involved on an equal basis, that they get the same consultation time and effort as other communities
- Understanding that consultation about how to consult and involve may be necessary
- Appreciating that there is likely to be suspicion and cynicism born of previous inadequate consultation
- Recognising sub-groups, such as young people, women and older people

with the addition of three specific ones:

- Ensuring that a range of methods and structures are applied which are sensitive to the varying traditions and cultures of the wide range of communities within the black and minority ethnic umbrella
- Appreciating that there is little history of consultation and involvement on an individual or community level with black and minority ethnic communities
- Recognising that for black and minority ethnic communities neighbourhood decline is not just about poverty, but also racial discrimination

For the majority of Neighbourhood Management schemes, therefore, effectively consulting with and actively involving black and minority ethnic communities at every level will again be breaking new ground. They will have to make concerted efforts to win the trust, respect and participation of black and minority ethnic communities. The good news is that black and minority ethnic communities have very real strengths which can assist the process of consultation and involvement. These are as follows:

- Strong networks in areas, and across tenures, which can relay information very quickly and effectively
- Strong cultural identities, which can focus activity, such as those around celebrations and events
- Strong faith identities, which can focus activity, such as those around prayers and places of worship

Faith-based regeneration in Hackney and Spitalfields, London

The North London Muslim Housing Association is being funded by a Housing Corporation IGP grant to pilot a faith based regeneration initiative in Hackney and Spitalfields in London. A survey of tenants in each area was undertaken to establish demographic diversity, the attitude of residents towards faith and to identify the specific needs of the areas. As part of the regeneration programme for each area, early specific activities have been implemented:

- a programme of neighbourhood based activities, including yoga, after school clubs, and classes for English as a second language
- training and employment projects in partnership with New Deal schemes and Employment Zones, with training tailored to the faith needs of individuals, such as time and space to pray

These schemes and others being planned are focused on local mosques and temples to utilise the huge potential capacity for expanding the range of activities and projects in and related to places of worship.

Practical suggestions for consultation and involvement include:

- Conducting a survey of black and minority ethnic residents or analysing all survey results by ethnicity
- Holding focus groups or community conferences that target different black and minority ethnic or faith groups
- Supporting and getting involved in community celebrations
- Helping to establish and support black and minority ethnic residents' groups
- Providing training and support for residents' groups to achieve equality goals
- Consulting black and minority ethnic RSLs and other organisations on how best to involve black and minority ethnic communities
- Providing capacity building and support for community groups
- Setting action plans with targets for the take-up of employment opportunities and other outputs of regeneration programmes

Source: Abstracted from the *Race and Housing Inquiry 2001*

- -

Resident-led consultation in Rochdale

In Rochdale, the local authority established a renewal area partnership with West Pennine and Ashiana Housing Associations and Surma Housing Co-operative. In the area, 74.4% of the community are of Asian origin, there are high levels of poverty and unemployment and some of the poorest housing and worst health indicators in the borough. Community involvement began in 1998 with a series of meetings and focus groups for women, young people, local businesses and community groups to identify problems and think about solutions. This led to:

- A community consultation event, bringing everyone together
- An open day, to display potential solutions
- A Community Consultation Panel, resident-led and comprising 12 residents, six local schools, three councillors, and two representatives each from women's groups, youth groups and local businesses

The 12 residents were elected, with every resident over eight years old able to vote, as 50% of the population in the area are under 16 years old. The Panel can vote on any plan or project proposed for the area as well as propose their own. There are sub-groups around business, women and girls, young people, health, the environment, training and employment and children.

Current priorities are to increase the percentage of Asian council tenants throughout the borough to 14% by 2011 and increase the proportion of Asian staff in the housing department, the long-term aim being to ensure that 14% of all new recruits are from the Asian communities.

- -

❑ Involving communities in rural areas

Neighbourhood Management, as a concept, fits well with renewal efforts in deprived urban neighbourhoods. Delivering it in rural areas and involving local communities in the process poses a very different challenge. It is one which a number of rural local authorities and registered social landlords are currently examining with some interest.

Rural areas have a number of disadvantages in delivering a Neighbourhood Management approach:

- Communities are smaller and more dispersed

- Communities of interest are often more important than communities of geography (although this can also be the case in urban areas)
- Social housing providers rarely have large stock holdings in individual neighbourhoods, villages or towns and lack the critical mass to make a significant impact on neighbourhood problems
- Many of the funding sources available for community initiatives in urban areas are not available in rural areas
- Community development workers and capacity building staff are very thin on the ground
- Resident and tenant involvement is under-developed in rural areas, compared with their urban counterparts

However, despite these substantial difficulties, there is growing interest amongst policy makers in tackling rural deprivation and a growing recognition that this is an increasingly important issue. Viable rural communities are critically dependent on maintaining a range of locally delivered services and are highly vulnerable to changes which occur without community involvement. The techniques and processes involved in managing rural neighbourhoods are, however, little different from those needed in urban areas.

Several registered social landlords with rural stock are examining interesting new ways of involving local communities in the future of their neighbourhoods. The Village Company concept (see case study in Chapter 3 – LHA) is one that is clearly capable of being replicated elsewhere. The Nottinghamshire companies have already created the basis for a Local Strategic Partnership with the various stakeholders and this presents real opportunities for local people to influence the way in which their whole community is managed and how services are provided.

❏ Community leadership

Some communities are already taking a lead role in developing Neighbourhood Management; others are being encouraged to do so through New Deal for Communities and other renewal programmes. These pilots will provide an important comparison with the agency-led approaches which are likely to form the majority of the initial round of pathfinders.

There are a number of potentially significant advantages in using community-led bodies to deliver Neighbourhood Management:

- They are more likely to be closely in tune with local needs and expectations than other bodies

- They can tackle local unemployment by targeting jobs they create specifically at the local community
- They can contract with major service providers to deliver certain local services themselves
- They can create community assets, against which they can borrow to sustain and enhance their neighbourhood role

Genuine community-led solutions to neighbourhood problems are relatively scarce in England, although there is no shortage of appropriate structures that they can adopt. As with all community-led bodies, accessing funding has often not been easy. Those that have successfully challenged the agency-led approach have often found it a long and arduous process, but the outcomes have usually been highly successful. Neighbourhood Management now offers an important opportunity to extend the various community leadership models across the country. These include the following:

- Community development trusts
- Tenant management organisations
- Tenant management co-ops
- Estate management boards
- Estate agreements
- Resident service organisations
- Local housing companies
- Neighbourhood forums and community-led partnerships

❏ Community development trusts

The sustainability of neighbourhoods depends heavily on local communities having an on-going role in their management. Community development trusts provide a vehicle for enabling communities to stop some of the assets created within their neighbourhoods leaking out into more affluent areas. Building up a local asset base potentially gives communities more control of their neighbourhoods, enabling them to provide local services themselves by raising capital to finance a range of initiatives.

Development trusts are increasingly being seen by stakeholders as one of the main exit strategies from neighbourhood renewal programmes and they certainly have a potentially major role to play in on-going Neighbourhood Management.

The Eldonians, Liverpool

Originally set up as a housing co-op by displaced City Council residents in the 1980s, the Eldonians has grown to become an outstanding example of how a neighbourhood can be transformed through community leadership.

As well as a community-based housing association, set up to build homes for 1000 residents, local people in Vauxhall have established a community development trust and a range of subsidiary companies, creating jobs for over 160 people. Working in partnership with a range of public and private sector organisations, the Eldonians have built their own village hall, a sports centre, a day nursery and a development of office and workshop units. They are about to start work on a mixed use enterprise park.

A successful community warden scheme has been up and running for nearly two years, with four permanent employees and 13 trainees tackling mainly anti-social behaviour and petty crime.

The real success of the Eldonians is not that all these activities are happening, but that they have been developed and managed by local people, not professional agencies. The investment in community assets has paid off, with the 'profits' recycled within the community and not leaking out into other areas.

❏ Tenant management organisations

Groups of tenants have been managing their own estates for many years – tenant management co-operatives have been around since the 1970s; estate management boards since the 1980s. Whatever their complexion, they have enabled tenants of public sector housing and, more recently, those in some registered social landlord stock, to take over some, or all, of the management responsibilities from their landlord, with devolved housing budgets and annually reviewed management agreements.

Tenant management organisations have had a good track record – they have generally been able to deliver a locally-based housing management service at a lower cost and a higher quality than their landlords could provide. They tend to depend heavily on extensive voluntary input from tenants themselves and substantial pump-priming financial support from DTLR and others.

●●

Burrowes Street Tenant Management Co-operative, Walsall

"We signed our management agreement in 1994. Rent arrears then were £18,609. In 1998 they were £7268 – 60% less and no-one has been taken to court. Repairs outstanding in 1994 were over 200; by 1996 they were all completed and now repairs are usually done the day they are reported"

Source: Abstracted from Proctor K (ed), (2000)

●●

❑ Estate management boards

Whilst tenant management co-operatives usually manage their homes themselves, estate management boards provide a halfway house, where tenants share responsibility with their landlords for estate management and maintenance. Some have expanded into a broader role.

●●

Bloomsbury Estate Management Board (EMB), Birmingham

Bloomsbury EMB has been in operation for 10 years and has delegated responsibility for the housing management budget on the estate. There are 12 tenants on a board of 20, representing 200 resident members. The Board is now responsible for managing its own contracts, under a management agreement with the local authority, who have four board members. Housing management spending is delegated to the Board by the local authority as part of the agreement.

The estate management board has now become a tenant management organisation, employs its own staff and there are plans to set up a residents' service organisation to tender in its own right for some estate services managed by the TMO. There are also plans to expand into the provision of other community services, including a cafe and park.

Source: Abstracted from Power A and Bergin E (1999)

●●

❑ Estate or neighbourhood agreements

Estate or neighbourhood agreements are a way of promoting greater local accountability for estate services, making policy issues more transparent at neighbourhood or estate level. They provide a contract between residents and agreed service standards, response times, targets and resources. Neighbourhood agreements are dealt with in more detail in Chapter 7.

❑ Resident service organisations

Resident service organisations, often linked to other forms of tenant management, provide opportunities for local training and job creation in such activities as communal gardening, environmental maintenance, caretaking, meals on wheels and so on.

Resident service organisations in Liverpool

CDS in Liverpool has set up a new regeneration company called INCLUDE. It will act as a contractor for the City Council, under a Public Service Agreement, and provide a range of neighbourhood services in Granby and Dingle.

INCLUDE and local agencies envisage setting up a pilot resident service organisation (RSO), believed to be unique in the UK. It will set up a community based social enterprise offering local jobs to deliver neighbourhood services for, by and with the local community. For example, work with the fire service will incorporate repairs to fire-damaged properties, the installation of smoke alarms and sprinklers to homes and innovative energy efficiency measures.

❑ Local housing companies

Local housing companies are public sector stock transfer vehicles which are being used predominantly in geographically compact urban areas. Many of them act as part of a group structure within an existing registered social landlord, but others are stand alone bodies, promoted by local authorities as an alternative to large scale voluntary transfer to an existing registered social landlord.

Most are constituted with boards comprising one third tenants, one third local authority councillors and one third independents, although a small number now have a resident majority. They offer a potentially key route for community leadership of neighbourhood renewal and management, particularly where their stock is compact, rather than dispersed, in communities with clear neighbourhood identities.

Local housing companies are almost always the largest stakeholders in their areas of operation. They should be able to develop a critical mass of assets which enables them to play a role in neighbourhood renewal and management which far exceeds that of a traditional social landlord. With support from their council partners, they have the ability to become virtually mini-local authorities within their neighbourhoods.

Community involvement in Poplar HARCA

Poplar HARCA is a local housing company, set up in 1998 to take over 5,000 homes from the London Borough of Tower Hamlets, following a successful tenant ballot. This part of east London has a long history of neighbourhood service delivery.

Around 200 residents are currently involved in the HARCA structure, which has divided the area into seven neighbourhoods, each with a neighbourhood centre and a locally-based Neighbourhood Management team.

Each neighbourhood has drawn up its own Community Plan and has an Estate Board, comprising only residents. They elect two tenants and one leaseholder to a joint Estate Panel covering the whole HARCA stock.

The Estate Panel elects seven resident directors to the HARCA Board. The Board has 18 members, including five councillors and six independents.

The HARCA places a strong emphasis on community-led renewal and Neighbourhood Management, delivered through community area directors and delivering a range of neighbourhood services, in partnership with other providers.

❑ Neighbourhood forums and community-led partnerships

Umbrella bodies, covering neighbourhoods of 4,000-5,000 homes and bringing local residents' organisations together to work more effectively, are a rarity in England. The development of Neighbourhood Management is likely to give this form of community leadership a substantial boost. The main front-runner of this approach is in Balsall Heath in Birmingham, where a combination of very local issues – rubbish in the street – and wider community issues – poor standards in local primary schools – galvanised various small residents' groups into creating an umbrella body for the whole neighbourhood.

Balsall Heath Neighbourhood Forum, Birmingham

Balsall Heath covers an area of 4,500 inner city homes. Neighbourhood Management here began from the bottom up, with residents endeavouring to discover how much was spent on local services in their neighbourhood and how they might control a small proportion of it.

They formed a resident-led Strategic Neighbourhood Partnership in 1996 with key public and private sector agencies.

At the instigation of the City Council chief executive, the Partnership set itself four main tasks in 1998:

1. To identify the locality budgets of the service providers and the degree of local discretion and/or influence over budget and service decisions
2. To identify the service and community boundaries in Balsall Heath and how different boundaries affect service provision
3. To review the mechanisms and processes for consultation used by each service provider and examine the opportunity to better co-ordinate and rejuvenate consultation
4. To form proposals for moving forward

A second three year Neighbourhood Development Plan has now been agreed and funding to support it is currently being sought from various sources.

The Forum itself has a turnover of nearly £250,000 a year, employs 15 staff, 11 of them local residents. They include a co-ordinator, two administrators, a senior safety, health, parenting and environmental trainer and four small teams of support workers for these activities.

Its Executive comprises 15 members, soon to be expanded to 19. From 2001, all 15 officers and ordinary members places are to be filled by local people, nominated and elected by residents' groups on an annual basis.

Although neighbourhood forums are a rarity, **community-led neighbourhood partnerships** are now beginning to emerge more widely, mainly in areas targeted for regeneration investment. They bring together key agencies and local people in a genuine partnership, but with the local community in control. They have a partnership board with a majority of elected residents and a community chair. The longer established neighbourhood partnerships have their own budgets and employ their own staff. In one or two cases, they act as their own accountable body for regeneration investment.

....

Royds Community Association, Bradford

Royds comprises three local authority housing estates, in south west Bradford, containing 3,350 homes and a population of 12,000 residents. The estates followed a familiar pattern of under-investment, and social and economic decline in the 1980s, something which City Challenge investment in the 1990s was unable to reverse.

Local action groups and residents' committees were formed and meetings held with the City Council and Government agencies. Four years of intensive campaigning led to the creation of a community association in 1994 and the award of a £31million seven year SRB programme in 1995, which has now become one of the country's most successful resident-led estate regeneration initiatives. Around £400,000 is spent annually on community capacity building.

Royds provides Neighbourhood Management at three levels:

1. Estate services provided by the community association rather than statutory agencies and employing local people (eg housing maintenance and repairs; landscaping services; a telephone research company)
2. Contract management for other service providers (eg management of a Healthy Living Centre on behalf of the local Primary Care Group)
3. Local service agreements with service providers (eg the provision of two community police officers)

Royds has a Partnering Charter with a wide range of public and private agencies, some of them represented on its Board. They include the City Council, local RSLs and developers involved in the regeneration programme.

Royds works on the basis that although it cannot expect to provide estate services at a cheaper rate than other service providers, it can manage these services much more effectively.

....

❏ Funding communities

Finding the funds needed to involve local communities in Neighbourhood Management is unlikely to be problematic for those initiatives in the initial two pilot rounds, or the 39 Round 1 and 2 New Deal for Communities programmes. Many of the Single Regeneration Budget Round 6 and some Round 5 programmes may also be able to allocate funds to this area as part of their Neighbourhood Management strategies. Elsewhere, however, community involvement will need to be funded through other Governmental and non-Governmental sources.

Sources of funding for community involvement in Neighbourhood Management

Neighbourhood Management pilots

Up to £700,000 a year is available for the pilot projects funded by Government. The community element of this package will vary between pilots, but as a general rule, at least **£120,000 a year** is likely to be needed for community capacity building in neighbourhoods of 4500-5000 households. This could be used to fund training and support programmes, employ community development staff and/or cover the running costs of a community-led neighbourhood board.

Community groups may also be able to access the new **£50million Community Chest**, distributed through government regional offices as part of the Neighbourhood Funding package. £50,000 will be available in each designated local authority, with grants of up to £5,000 available for individual community projects. Detailed guidance was not available from Government at the time of writing.

The **Community Empowerment Fund**, administered by Government Offices, is specifically aimed at achieving effective and meaningful involvement of communities and the voluntary sector in LSPs. **£36 million** is available over the next three years. Although this fund cannot be used directly for Neighbourhood Management work with communities, many of the processes involved – outreach work, training, support, and information dissemination – will overlap.

Potential sources include those set out in the accompanying table – brief details of each programme are included in Appendix 2.

Community trusts and foundations, community foundations and registered social landlords are also potential sources of funding support for communities involved in Neighbourhood Management initiatives outside the pilot areas. Details of these can also be found in Appendix 2.

Potential sources of funding for communities

Government departments
DTLR *Tenant Empowerment Grant* programme
Home Office's *Community Resource Fund*
Department for Education and Skills *Community Champions Fund*
Department for Education and Skills *Neighbourhood Support Fund*
Department for Education and Skills *Millennium Volunteers*

Government sponsored public sector agencies
Regional Development Agencies *Community Investment Fund*
Housing Corporation *Community Training and Enabling Grants*
Regional Offices of the NHS Executive *Health Action Zones*
Education Action Zones and Sure Start programmes, administered by the
Department for Education and Skills

Local authorities
Grant funding for community organisations

European funding programmes
European Regional Development Fund
Urban Initiative
European Social Fund

National Lottery programmes
The Community Fund – *Community Involvement; Poverty and Disadvantage; Awards for All*
The New Opportunities Fund
The Arts Council *Arts for Everyone*

CHAPTER 5

DEVELOPING CAPACITY IN HOUSING ORGANISATIONS

What this Chapter is about

This chapter looks at the changes which will be necessary in housing organisations to enable them to engage effectively in Neighbourhood Management, including:

- Ways of achieving cultural change
- Finding a balance between core functions and involvement in Neighbourhood Management
- The need for new types of leadership

'Building institutional capacity to plan and deliver a community-based approach to neighbourhood regeneration…is as vital a component to achieving sustainable regeneration of the poorest neighbourhoods as is building the capacity of the communities themselves…all the capacity building in the world will count for very little if doors are not open and those who have access to the money and power are not listening.'

Source: Duncan & Thomas (2000a)

Neighbourhood Management will not happen unless the organisations involved are geared up for it and have the capacity to deliver. For most local authorities and RSLs, organisational change is nothing new. The need for cultural change is increasingly being recognised, but not yet always acted upon. Few have yet embarked on a complete review of the financial and budgetary mechanisms for service delivery.

This chapter also looks at the need to establish a baseline for organisations to assess the necessary changes and the role they can play in Neighbourhood Management. It considers the balancing of Neighbourhood Management activity with core functions. It looks at the implications of stock rationalisation through management and ownership transfers.

It considers the new types of leadership that will be required and the changes needed to achieve the breaking down of departmental barriers.

❑ Cultural and organisational change

One of the key challenges to delivering successful Neighbourhood Management is the requirement for cultural and organisational change. The main elements of Neighbourhood Management depend upon comprehensive change within the statutory organisations and agencies which currently control service delivery in deprived neighbourhoods. It will be necessary to transfer significant control and resources from the central to a local level. Communities will need support to achieve the degree of power they want. The process will require truly integrated working between a wide range of organisations and service providers. For many organisations, this will mean nothing short of thorough institutional reform.

The ethos of the paternalistic delivery of public services upon which local government was established is no longer appropriate. Indeed, it has come to inhibit social development. The origins of the housing association movement emerged, on the whole, from a more altruistic approach so it could be argued that, for RSLs, there is less distance to travel. For both, however, new conditions and expectations will require new forms of social and political management.

Chapter 2 considers the changes at Government level, the Modernising Government programme and individual departmental change programmes which are being implemented. In addition, in the context of neighbourhood renewal, the National Strategy detailed several measures to start to change cultures within Government departments:

- Each Government department with responsibility for policies that affect deprived neighbourhoods will be developing targets for interchange with organisations working in deprived neighbourhoods, and particularly those working with minority ethnic groups
- Government will consider the merits of sponsoring a special Charter Mark award for services in deprived areas, and will look at social exclusion issues as part of the review of Charter Mark criteria. Consideration will also be given to an Investors in Communities scheme (see Chapter 6) or a Community Mark
- The existing network of departmental 'Consumer Champions' will be engaged in improving the responsiveness of services in deprived areas
- Consideration will be given to developing a People's Panel that is focused explicitly on deprived areas

❑ Change at the local level

At a local level, for local authorities and housing associations, the pressures for change will require a considerably more extensive, and speedier, response. And one which is way beyond the current requirements of the modernisation agenda and Best Value, important though these are. The danger is that the reform necessary for Neighbourhood Management will be focused on technical change involving internal structures and procedures, along with education and training to re-skill professionals. Whilst these changes are critical, they must be part of a cultural change, which is much more reliant upon areas such as strong leadership, attitudes, and approaches. These are the things that will really change the ethos of an organisation, its spirit and beliefs – a move away from a public service ethos to that of a public innovation ethos.

Changing the ethos

Public service ethos	Public innovation ethos
Concern for procedures (fairness, propriety)	Concern for results (quality, efficiency, impact)
Controlling (central accountability, risk avoidance)	Steering (clear guidance, local autonomy, valuing staff)
Conformance (obedience, reliability)	Performance (creativity and inventiveness, risk-taking)
Consistency (uniformity, equity)	Diversity (responsive to differences, customised, flexibility)
Traditional councillor roles (policy making, service decision making, constituent concerns)	New roles for councillors (as strategists, monitors of performance, community advocates)
Service the public (listen to and respond to the public)	New roles for the local authority (empowering consumers, citizens, communities)

Source: Hambleton et al (1997)

But how can the ethos of an organisation change? What are the incentives to pursue change? And what practical steps are needed to start the process?

❏ The business case for change

It is anticipated that housing organisations will want to change because it is a vital pre-condition to achieving successful Neighbourhood Management and social inclusion, and to meeting the changing expectations of residents and local communities generally. However, there are also tangible business benefits to attract those organisations which remain sceptical or inert:

- Ensuring that the communities where housing organisations hold assets are sustainable (that they are places where people want to live)
- Increasing customer satisfaction levels
- Reducing turnover rates
- Reducing void rates
- Reducing rent arrears
- Enabling housing organisations to target resources at priority issues for residents
- Meeting the requirements of Best Value

These direct benefits, which impact on the balance sheet of an organisation, are further enhanced by indirect benefits. As well as having a clear social impact, indirect benefits create a virtuous circle by themselves supporting the specific work and objectives of individual housing organisations by:

- Increasing tenant empowerment
- Helping to increase economic regeneration
- Helping to reduce crime and the fear of crime
- Helping to develop partnership arrangements with other agencies providing services to an estate or neighbourhood

Source: Adapted from Aldbourne Associates (2001)

❏ Black and minority ethnic RSLs

Changing cultures to meet the requirements of neighbourhood renewal and management requires a somewhat different approach for black and minority ethnic housing organisations. In the need to change cultures, they start from a different place.

In some respects, they are a few steps ahead of the majority of mainstream housing organisations. Black and minority ethnic RSLs have emerged as a direct response to the unmet housing and cultural needs of black and minority ethnic communities. As such, they are still focused on empowering local communities and delivering services which are strongly influenced by local need. Given their youth most have not yet become remote, professionalised bureaucracies.

For most black and minority ethnic RSLs, the organisational changes necessary will be focused on integrated working with a wide range of other organisations and service providers. While these can be addressed internally, in the same way as for mainstream housing organisations, black and minority ethnic RSLs are starting from a few steps back. Their marginalisation away from the mainstream housing sector means that they have much less experience of inter-agency partnerships; they have to contend with widespread racist attitudes; and their independence can be threatened by the pressures for mergers and stock rationalisation.

The Race and Housing Inquiry 2001 is a partnership of the Commission for Racial Equality, the National Housing Federation, the Federation of Black Housing Organisations and the Housing Corporation. It was established to identify the practical ways in which race equality policy objectives could be translated into tangible action and outcomes. Responses from the housing sector include some general suggestions for building the capacity of black and minority ethnic RSLs which have a clear relationship to Neighbourhood Management:

- Establish action plans for supporting black and minority ethnic RSLs, including the provision of advice, training and development agent services
- Agree fair development partnership arrangements with black and minority ethnic RSLs
- Establish a development protocol between RSLs and local authorities, that establish the involvement of black and minority ethnic RSLs
- Employ black and minority ethnic RSLs as advisers
- Develop secondment opportunities to and from black and minority ethnic RSLs

Source: *Race and Housing Inquiry* (2001)

The case for change has been set out but how can organisations make it happen?

❏ Joining up

Marilyn Taylor, professor of social policy at Brighton University, in her influential study *Top down meets bottom up* takes the joining up element of Neighbourhood Management as the focus around which cultural change can be implemented and managed. She argues that, to date, joining up has been at a level, whereby partners are allowed to maintain their individual authority while co-operating on some issues (often those that are marginal to their main business). Neighbourhood Management will require collaboration, where partners pool authority and resources, as well as share risk. The implications of this approach for organisations are:

- Strong leadership within organisations and agencies, with senior officers and politicians fully committed to joined up working, which is driven down through all levels, particularly middle managers and front-line staff
- New skills, careers and professional approaches
- New ways of sharing knowledge and enabling clear communication up, down and across organisations
- Accepting risk as part of change, and failure as part of learning, adopting new frameworks for performance measurement, regulation, audit and risk management
- Allowing enough time for change, encouraging 'quick wins' to illustrate change but not quick fixes
- Procedures which enable joined up accountability, jointly agreed joined up information systems, action plans and outcomes
- Inculcating a community-based approach to all aspects of organisational structures, procedures and programmes
- Linking joined up working to local jobs and community assets to broaden the impact of Neighbourhood Management

Source: Adapted from Taylor, M (2000b)

There will also be the need to agree and implement joined up performance indicators.

Therefore, for the great majority of housing organisations, the joining up element will present a huge challenge to current ways of working, managing and operating. Communities will have to build capacity in order to strengthen their individual and collective abilities to take more control of their lives and their communities, but housing organisations will also need to do the same on a corporate basis. This will help identify gaps and weaknesses. It will indicate the extent of the role they could play in Neighbourhood Management and assess their ability to lead or support the process.

The first step is establishing where the gaps and weaknesses are, as well as the existing strengths. A self-audit of organisational capacity is a useful first step, assessing what needs to change in the organisation to enable it to operate successfully in the Neighbourhood Management field.

❏ Capacity building plans

A capacity building plan could include the following components:

- A vision and commitment to change agreed at councillor/board level
- Interpretation and implementation on a day to day basis by senior management
- Organisational re-structuring to change from departmental issue-based working to multi-disciplinary area-based working
- An organisational capacity building plan defining what gaps/weaknesses need addressing and what strengths need building on
- An organisational development plan detailing the learning, training and skills needs of all staff and councillors/board members, which includes a requirement to work on the front-line
- Development of an open access plan to encourage residents into the organisation
- Development of a race equality action plan covering service delivery and employment practices
- Individual professional development plans to ensure career progression
- A review of staff composition and levels to ensure black and minority ethnic staff are supported, and recruited, as necessary
- A review of staff levels and grades to ensure that front-line staff have the necessary status
- A review of pay structures to ensure that front-line staff are properly remunerated
- A menu of incentives to encourage staff to work differently
- A review of committee/board structures to ensure strong representation by users

The question of the scale and speed of change is critical here – how much needs doing and should it be done incrementally or comprehensively?

❏ Implementing change

Approaching change will depend in part on the extent to which housing organisations intend to change to tackle neighbourhood regeneration and management. For some, the best approach will be to set up specialist teams within their existing structure and recruit staff with appropriate skills.

Others will be making more fundamental changes to their organisations to become social regeneration agencies, where all the staff will be expected to absorb the new culture and acquire new skills. This latter approach is likely to be more appealing to those housing providers who already have significant demand and social problems within their own stock.

Changing internal structures, LHA

In recent years, LHA has replaced traditional sub-committees of the Board with 3 regional boards, the boundaries of which were the same as those of the local authorities. These are tenant-led and this has directly resulted in a re-organisation of investment priorities to better reflect tenant priorities, as well as local community action plans which set the agenda for change and upon which investment decisions are based.

'Whatever the extent of the change, what will be required is a mixture of structural and cultural measures. This could mean combining 'strong' measures, i.e. regulation, financial incentives and sanctions, with 'weak' tools, i.e. persuasion, information, systems of learning and building networks.'

Source: Adapted from Perri 6, Leat D, Seltzer K and Stoker G (1999)

The weak tools are more important but also take longer to implement, so an incremental approach is likely to be more successful. It would also have the advantage of being more palatable to existing staff, giving it a greater degree of likely success.

Such an approach could be built upon:

- Existing initiatives, such as housing stock transfers, community plans, Best Value
- Small packages of services, such as environmental services and housing, or crime and health
- Existing partnerships, such as schools and local health providers, or local police and tenant management organisations

An incremental approach, however, should not be interpreted as a way of limiting change. Rather, it is a process towards achieving comprehensive change that is:

- More manageable
- Less threatening to staff
- Gives time for partnerships to move from informal to formal arrangements
- Allows the doubters to see how it works and join in
- Enables the testing out of ideas and practices for adoption or rejection
- Gives time for review and appraisal of progress, allowing for change and refinement

Fundamental to change will be strong leadership. While Neighbourhood Management is a way of working and should not depend upon individuals, leadership is an important aspect. Driving through change will require vision, commitment, the ability to motivate and inspire, and take hard decisions. It will also demand leaders who can lead by example, who themselves can change and adapt, interpreting change as an opportunity rather than a threat. It will be their role to encourage others to do likewise.

❑ Leadership

New organisations and cultures will require new forms of leadership. The report from PAT 16, *Learning Lessons*, defines 'entrepreneurship' as the key characteristic of the professionals, community leaders, board members and councillors who will be leading Neighbourhood Management.

PAT16 concluded that entrepreneurs are invariably people with ideas and a purpose in search of assets and resources. They discover and put into practice opportunities to create value by meeting unmet needs or finding a better way to deliver a product or service. Successful entrepreneurship also has to be a team effort; it needs a team of skilled and committed people to make things happen.

Clearly, effective leadership also requires political support. An alliance between political leaders and public sector managers is a vital element, particularly given the risks involved in doing things in new ways epitomised by Neighbourhood Management.

More particularly, it will require a recognition of the tension between strong leadership and local accountability through devolved management and budgets. The best civic leaders will be those who can provide vision, direction and support at a strategic level and 'let go' at the local level. This requires the ability to encourage and enable self-determination by locally-based staff and communities by providing support at the corporate, partnership and political levels through:

- Accessing financial resources
- Identifying and making available administrative and staff resources
- Troubleshooting
- Finding ways through financial, legislative, and procedural barriers
- Acting as advocates
- Continually re-emphasising racial equality
- Taking a small operational role, being 'hands-off'
- Negotiating and developing policies

The characteristics of entrepreneurs

- Adopting innovative ways of tackling social problems
- Challenging traditional ways of working
- Bringing together ideas, resources and people to instigate change
- Spotting opportunities and making use of underused resources
- Taking risks and
- Responding to a problem with a clear outcome in mind – a can-do philosophy

Combined with more traditional leadership skills:
- Understanding others' perspectives
- Bringing others on board to change things
- Making things happen
- Motivating and inspiring others
- Building a consensus
- Sharing lessons and information
- Securing community support for solutions
- Taking hard decisions and not fudging issues

Source: Social Exclusion Unit (2000e)

Although these characteristics may, at first sight, appear to call for super heroes or heroines, the reality is likely to be rather more pragmatic. The most important strength a civic leader can have is a belief in what they are doing, a conviction that there is a better way of doing things. In terms of Neighbourhood Management, this means a clear and unequivocal commitment to the key principles of better services, community empowerment and cultural change.

❑ Integrating Neighbourhood Management with core functions

Neighbourhood Management requires the effective co-ordination of a large number of agencies and services. In neighbourhoods where social housing is divided between several landlords, the task is made more difficult. In some cities, it is not unusual to find up to a dozen RSLs with stock in an urban neighbourhood of 5,000 dwellings. This is a product of many years of competitive bidding for Housing Corporation resources following the abandonment of 'zoning', which gave individual RSLs exclusive rights to purchase or build homes in geographical areas.

Joint management agreements in such neighbourhoods are relatively rare. Each RSL and the local authority services their own stock with their own staff or contract arrangements. In organisational terms, it may make sense for each landlord but in neighbourhood terms and, from a community perspective, it is likely to be seen as highly inefficient and inappropriate.

There are consequently bound to be inherent tensions for many social housing landlords between management of large portfolios of dispersed stock and meeting the local accountability and service efficiency demands of Neighbourhood Management.

There is growing interest amongst some local authorities and RSLs in a radical solution to this problem – reducing the number of social landlords in neighbourhoods, through a process of stock rationalisation. Neighbourhood-based transfers of local authority stock to existing or newly-formed RSLs, and stock-swops between RSLs, enabling them to focus their management effort in fewer neighbourhoods without reducing their portfolios, is now on the agenda.

Stock rationalisation in Liverpool

The City has recently been zoned for housing purposes, with lead status given to nine RSLs for particular neighbourhoods. The City is two thirds of the way through this process at present. Each lead RSL will work with the City to develop sustainable housing solutions and joint approaches to allocations, investment and management. Some of them may need to restructure. There will be extensive property swops and demolition. Stock transfer ballots are due in October/November 2001 and will be zone based – there will be no citywide transfer ballot.

All the 35,000-strong council housing stock will be transferred to the neighbourhood RSLs incrementally (subject to the ballots) chosen on their ability to act as a regeneration vehicle, not just as a housing provider.

The relationship between the City Council and RSLs is crucial to the success of the programme. They are being expected to re-engineer their businesses and re-focus on the City as part of the deal.

Creating critical mass in neighbourhoods – where a large proportion of the housing stock and perhaps other assets are owned and controlled by one social landlord – has potentially significant advantages for the Neighbourhood Management process. For this reason, if no other, RSLs set up as local housing companies or community based housing associations in geographically focused areas arguably have the best chance of making a success of Neighbourhood Management. RSLs without this strong neighbourhood focus will have to work much harder to make a significant impact and much will depend on how well they are organised at neighbourhood level.

❏ Multi-disciplinary working

The dilemma of whether to build specialist or generic capacity at organisational or individual level is a long running debate amongst housing professionals. Neighbourhood Management gives it a clear focus. Generic teams will be required which are capable of operating in a variety of settings, comprising individuals with areas of specialism. The development of multi-disciplinary project teams rather than single issue programme teams is a fundamental requirement of Neighbourhood Management.

This will require internal re-organisation and the creation of practical working links across different sectors and agencies. It will involve different working practices. Many meetings and events will be outside of the normally accepted working day, in venues and locations that may be far from ideal. It will require greater willingness to work with organisations typically scorned or mistrusted by public sector staff, such as private landlords, small businesses and informal groups of residents.

Most SRB and all NDC programmes have already established partnership boards with multi-agency representation, albeit largely driven, overtly or covertly, by the local authority. Those housing organisations that are setting up new regeneration companies have created boards with a much greater community presence and control.

The ability to treat these partners as equals and be prepared to invest time and money in building confidence and capacity, are essential to effective neighbourhood regeneration and management.

Neighbourhood Management will require pooled budgets and close working together of staff from different public service providers, such as social services, health and the police. Experience to date shows that it has often been difficult to build up an element of trust and shared objectives between these, and other, agencies. If service level agreements (which devolve responsibility to the community for the management of budgets and the delivery of services) are to work, the skills of the Neighbourhood Management teams to achieve will be crucial.

Multi-disciplinary neighbourhood teams – Liverpool

Liverpool City Council has a Neighbourhood Management Unit as part of Neighbourhood Services. The Unit is currently piloting neighbourhood services in six areas of the city, each with 4-5,000 homes. Each area has a team leader and co-ordinator. There has been a deliberate policy to recruit staff from a wide range of backgrounds and with a variety of skills. Currently, they include people from:

- An independent mediation service
- The city's anti-social behaviour unit
- A college of further education
- The city's environmental maintenance section
- The city's private sector renewal section
- Credit unions
- The City's housing department

Managing multi-disciplinary teams also requires particular skills, which are probably more familiar to many housing staff following Best Value reviews and other recent initiatives requiring a joined up approach across organisations. Nevertheless, training in this area will still be required for most staff moving into Neighbourhood Management roles.

Housing organisations will have to recognise the need to value people who have a different kind of career, moving across agencies, sectors and departments rather than progressing through the ranks in the same sector in the traditional manner. Recent research from Demos (an independent think tank and research institute) has coined the term 'pinball careers' to describe this new type of approach.

Some ideas for rewarding cross-boundary working

- Building a second expertise/experience into every senior manager/civil servant's job-plan
- Encouraging secondments, job swapping and shadowing
- Requiring experience in other departments/agencies for all appointments above a certain level and, at the least, not penalising cross-boundary workers for their failure to keep within departmental boundaries
- Recruiting 'poachers turned gamekeepers', i.e. encouraging the interchange of staff between purchasers/commissioners and providers/suppliers

Source: Leat, D (2000)

❑ Pooling budgets

Pooling budgets across departments and organisations is one of the key elements in Neighbourhood Management. It is vital to promoting effective multi-disciplinary working. It provides the strongest signal that there is a commitment to a truly, and not token, joined up approach. It is also a complex and difficult process. It requires organisations to change their value systems from seeing control as equating to how much money they have, to how much it can buy. In other words, putting greater value on the impact that can be achieved through budget pooling, on the outputs rather than the input.

If pooling budgets is to work administratively and conceptually, it requires:

- A commitment to a joined up approach and trust between organisations and individuals
- Shared objectives
- Joined up accountability structures
- Workable inter-agency and inter-departmental agreements setting out financial commitments
- Identification of procedures, rules and regulations which need to be made flexible or changed
- A consideration of ring-fencing for high-risk services, i.e. minority needs
- Agreement about the use of savings
- Staff developing financial accountability to a collection of organisations/departments rather than simply the formal employer

The structural ways in which budgets might be pooled are addressed in Chapter 7, although it should be borne in mind that experience in this area is very limited at present.

❑ Implications for staff

The implications for staff engaged in organisational change are, of course, significant. Organisational and cultural change will require new forms of learning as well as new approaches to delivery. How this is approached and implemented could make or break the successful transition of housing organisations from departmentally driven service providers to multi-disciplinary regeneration vehicles.

Much will depend upon staff development and learning being part of the ethos of housing organisations. It will require an understanding of what the personal and professional barriers are to development and learning. This will need to be combined with a positive and supportive approach to providing appropriate and accessible forms of learning. The aim should be to liberate staff to develop areas of interest and expertise which will enhance their skills and knowledge, open up career opportunities and encourage personal development.

Organisations will also have to strike a delicate balance between support for staff to adapt to change and sanctions for refusal and inertia. The most common reaction to change is defensiveness. The most successful approach is likely to be clear sanctions which are reserved for situations where drastic action is required (Stewart, 1999).

❑ Black and minority ethnic staff

Organisational and cultural change for Neighbourhood Management should encompass the massive cultural shift required in the housing sector, and elsewhere, to achieve race equality. This is particularly the case for mainstream white-led housing organisations. The majority need to change the culture of their organisations to one that recognises and maximises the potential of its entire workforce. This will mean bringing equality issues to the centre of their service provision, rather than remaining at the fringe of their activities. Many black and minority ethnic staff struggle with racism in the workplace and evidence from *A Question of Diversity: black and minority staff in the RSL sector*, indicates that there are limited opportunities for black and minority ethnic staff even though they tended to be more qualified than white staff.

White led RSLs have much to learn from black and minority ethnic RSLs who have equal proportions of black and minority ethnic and white staff within their organisations. The Race Relations Amendment Act 2000 creates a new general duty on public authorities such as local authorities to promote race equality and avoid race discrimination before it occurs.

The Housing Corporation will be responsible for ensuring that RSLs effectively comply with the duties contained in the legislation.

It will therefore be important for all housing organisations to ensure that the changes necessary for Neighbourhood Management are accompanied by concerted action on equality. The Race and Housing Inquiry 2001 submissions included the following suggestions:

- Set targets, monitor and review performance on staff recruitment, turnover, promotion and training by ethnicity

- Establish non-discriminatory recruitment procedures, for example, representative interviewing panels or competency/assessment based approaches
- Provide opportunities for secondments, mentoring, fast track training and acting up either targeted at black and minority ethnic staff or more generally
- Develop links with schools, colleges and community groups and hold recruitment fairs to encourage black and minority ethnic people to join the sector
- Have employment practices that allow for observance of religious practices
- Conduct staff surveys and analyse the results by ethnicity
- Support black and minority ethnic staff groups

Other measures could also be considered. Black and minority ethnic staff may need to have a safe person, either within the organisation or externally that they can feedback inequality issues to and receive support from without feeling compromised and all staff should receive black and minority ethnic training and awareness guidance on induction to their jobs and continuously afterwards.

Further recommendations for a programme for action are detailed in *A Question of Diversity: black and minority ethnic staff in the RSL sector*, The Housing Corporation.

A further proposal is to develop an independent award, quality standard or accreditation scheme for good practice in race and housing. This might be based on Investors in People and take a similar approach to the Investors in Communities model currently being tested.

CHAPTER 6

DEVELOPING COMPETENCIES, SKILLS AND KNOWLEDGE IN PROFESSIONALS

What this Chapter is about

This chapter looks at what housing professionals will require in terms of new skills and knowledge to meet the challenges of Neighbourhood Management and what it will mean for the traditional housing profession, including:

- The impact of the changing environment on housing managers
- How professionals can learn new tricks
- Sources of advice and guidance

'It is not just that good policies are called for, the culture change requires good people.'

Source: Atkinson, D (2000)

Joining up services, community leadership and effective partnership working will require professionals to work in ways which will be new to many. The local authority or RSL will no longer be the controlling body, but will be there to facilitate and support new groups and individuals from the community and from other agencies to deliver services and initiatives.

Housing professionals will need to change in response to the introduction of Neighbourhood Management. For those interested in becoming neighbourhood managers there is likely to be a particularly steep learning curve.

❏ Learning and development – a changing environment

The PAT 16 Report *Learning Lessons*, recognises that… *'the housing service has a pivotal role to play in neighbourhood renewal. Of all public services it tends to have the strongest link with the deprived communities living in social housing.'* It is likely, therefore, that housing professionals will play a central role in delivering Neighbourhood Management. What is likely to be different is that many of them will not necessarily be housing managers any more.

There is a strong feeling in the sector that, although there will clearly continue to be housing management tasks to perform, the standard role of housing manager will change enormously or even disappear. Although there is, as yet, no coherent view of exactly what will happen, there is a consensus emerging on the approach and attributes that will be necessary. These include:

- The ability to work in an enabling rather than directing way – wherever possible, to advise and guide, not manage and control
- The ability to work across sectors, with different organisational styles and cultures, for a boss who may be from another service sector
- The willingness to start from the community's agenda and not that of agencies
- The ability to work in a way which builds community capacity, implicitly requiring the diminution of their own power
- The ability to work with groups and organisations over which they have no authority or control
- The willingness to trust non-professionals
- The courage to devolve responsibility to people and organisations largely unknown to them
- The confidence to take risks and find innovative ways of doing things
- The confidence to work on the front-line rather than the back-room
- The ability to work flexibly and informally
- Tenacity, self-reliance and self-motivation
- Influencing skills, developing consensus and the ability to work with communities and service providers to create and promote a vision for the area
- Leadership skills

The common thread running through the current re-evaluation of the role of housing and other professionals is the need to change the balance of power with local residents. It could be said that professionalism has become an end in itself, rather than an accumulation of knowledge and expertise which is offered to the service of the community. The relationship with residents has, therefore, become distorted to such an extent that many professionals are seen as gatekeepers, placing barriers in the way of residents rather than using their skills to find solutions. The ensuing hostility and suspicion that many professionals experience is the direct result.

Several years of Single Regeneration Budget (SRB) rounds and other initiatives have brought some housing professionals into closer contact with residents. They have also had to become more involved in strategic and local partnerships with a wide range of individuals and agencies, including residents. In all these areas, however, the local authority has invariably had a controlling role.

More recently, the New Deal for Communities programme has tried to put communities in the lead, and in many cases this is working, albeit slowly and sometimes painfully. Even here, however, the local authority usually has an influential role as the accountable body, responsible for the money and therefore able, at least in principle, to veto and control. Neighbourhood Management boards are unlikely to give the local authority the same degree of influence – they are unlikely to have a majority or controlling interest at all.

This will require staff to have very different skills from those necessary for the running of a traditional housing team or department where roles and status are clearly defined, the duties reasonably understood and mapped out, with the corporate entity of the local authority or RSL providing legal and other back up services. These are likely to include skills in:

- Building networks
- Negotiating and mediating
- Assimilating best practice
- Financial management
- Creative problem solving – 'thinking outside the box'
- Team working
- Project development and management
- Communication

Perhaps worryingly for many housing professionals, there is a view emerging that Neighbourhood Management staff are unlikely to be recruited from local authority housing departments or RSLs. Too often, it is felt, housing professionals think they already do a form of Neighbourhood Management, which will merely have to be tweaked to fit the new agenda. In reality they operate a landlord service at neighbourhood level. Changing the tenant/landlord relationship will be fundamental to the success of Neighbourhood Management – perpetuating it will strangle it at birth.

If current housing staff are to meet the challenges of Neighbourhood Management, particularly in building relationships with local communities, they will have to:

- Stake out their independence from local authorities and RSLs
- Visibly break free of old allegiances/employers
- Transform the landlord/tenant relationship
- Make it clear their priority is people not properties
- Create a balance between getting too close and maintaining the traditional professional 'arms length' approach

Housing professionals may have some of the skills but they need to convince potential employers within the neighbourhood renewal arena that they have these skills and abilities. At present, many employers are looking for people with attitudes and approaches more akin to those of a community development worker who has run their own business, or who has worked in the private sector, but has a social conscience. Some employers take the view that professional qualifications are not as important as people who are adaptable and flexible. The need for the right approach is increasingly over-riding the requirement for professional qualifications. Put bluntly, employers are tending to seek out the skills they need in the wider market-place rather than looking automatically to the recognised professions.

The question is will they find those skills in the wider market-place?

Indeed, the very early indications from RSLs and local authorities are that neighbourhood staff and the chief executives of community regeneration organisations are being recruited from urban regeneration rather than housing management backgrounds because of their experience of working in multi-agency environments.

The evidence is that there are plenty of people, particularly new graduates, wanting to work in the regeneration sector. There are also plenty of new jobs, many of which can't be filled because there are not yet enough experienced professionals to go around. Both graduates and current staff in housing organisations will require further training and experience in the skills needed. To compound the problems, too many local authorities and RSLs are still only offering short-term contracts to regeneration staff, along with, arguably, levels of pay which are too low. Yet they expect to recruit people who have innovative, people-based, getting-things-done skills, and who are financially astute.

❏ Capacity building for professionals – the challenges

How do individuals respond to these challenges? The PAT 16 report observed that *'professionals are often not equipped to operate effectively in poor neighbourhoods'*. It envisages the need for *'improved basic training within professions and making training more relevant to the challenges of working in deprived neighbourhoods'*. The recent subtle shifts in language from education and training to skills and knowledge indicate a change in the process and content of future student and staff development.

Job titles such as neighbourhood manager, neighbourhood officer or assistant, and neighbourhood warden are emerging thick and fast and will inevitably form the basis of a new professional structure. But it will also have to encompass a redefinition of being professional if it is not to perpetuate the present divisions and barriers between the community and neighbourhood staff. One of the important requirements of these new staff is their ability and willingness to relate to and work alongside community organisations and residents, for whom the trappings of current professional status and culture are often an anathema.

Until very recently, little, if any, attention has been given to capacity building for professionals. While building capacity in communities is now an accepted part of neighbourhood regeneration, what has been largely overlooked is that one of the key ways in which this will happen is through building capacity in professionals. This is now changing. The areas which have been identified by PAT 16 as weak in the skills and knowledge base of professionals already working within regeneration agencies are:

Weaknesses in skills and knowledge amongst professionals

- Poor knowledge of research into what works and under what circumstances
- Failure to effectively use key processes: problem solving, option appraisal, action planning, etc.
- Lack of rigour in project management
- Insufficient priority and outcome setting
- Poor examples of partnership working
- Insufficient use of effective ways of strengthening community institutions.

Source: Social Exclusion Unit (2000e)

In their defence, these gaps do not only apply to housing professionals – they are found across all sectors. In the housing sector, most housing management staff work within well defined areas of responsibility and within established systems. Neighbourhood regeneration and management will require much broader skills and practical applications of experience, much of which is beyond the normal day-to-day experience of many housing professionals.

❏ The content and process of learning

A survey of employers' views has ranked the most important change areas for housing professionals over the next five years.

Important change areas for housing professionals

- Stock changes
- Quality, performance, Best Value
- Information and communications technology
- Social exclusion and regeneration
- Customer, consumer and community focus
- Increasing complexity and diversity
- Changed organisational arrangements
- Inter-agency, generic, cross-cutting and multi-skilling issues
- The changing government policy agenda

Abstracted from Reid, B, Hills, S and Kane, S (2000)

Along with the content of what they learn, the ways in which professionals actually learn is also changing. Instead of training providers taking the lead, increasingly organisations are opting to build capacity through their own organisational development strategies, using a pick and mix, custom-built approach to training their staff. This is a clear departure from the traditional approach, as it is needs-led and organisationally rather than sectorally centred, reflecting some of the key principles of Neighbourhood Management itself. Such an approach may include a mix of:

- One-off courses run externally
- In-house delivery of one-off training events
- Day release or distance learning
- Customised products developed in house
- Customised products developed in partnership with external training bodies

The delivery might be through:

- A tailored learning programme devised and implemented at neighbourhood level
- Specific training for individual professions
- Mixed-group learning
- Support for individual learning
- Tapping into national and regional learning opportunities
- Accessing expert advice
- Residents training professionals

❑ Learning new tricks

This approach will impact on individuals, enabling them to access tailored courses which suit their level of expertise and personal/work circumstances. The new content is likely to be a combination of skills and competence-based needs together with information-based education and training. That is a balance of content (factual areas that should be covered) to approach (how to go about doing things, methods of delivery, types of product). In addition, new-style skills and knowledge development will have to promote the all round development of the individual, both to achieve personal development and produce the people necessary to achieve the all round approach required in Neighbourhood Management.

Joint training, across sectors and involving communities, is becoming more common. It is extremely useful in developing understanding and awareness, disseminating knowledge and sharing best practice. Communities in particular can play an important role in building the capacity of professionals:

- Generating examples of good practice – first hand experience of what works and what does not
- Advising on the application of good practice – how to implement a particular approach in different circumstances
- Disseminating their first hand experiences of living in deprived neighbourhoods
- Providing capable, experienced individuals to act as advisers/mentors
- Identifying key skills gaps in individuals, professions and across professions
- Assisting directly in training for professionals

Residents for Regeneration

Based at the Balsall Heath Forum, Residents for Regeneration (R4R) is a group of residents with direct personal experience at the coalface of regeneration. Supported by a small team of professionals, it offers support services to residents in other parts of the country, and to public sector agencies wishing to move from doing to enabling. They offer a package which includes:

- Exchange visits, with R4R consultants visiting residents/ professionals to offer advice and reciprocal visits to Balsall Heath
- A tracking report, detailing the outcomes of the visits
- Support material, comprising a DIY kit of information and guidance with training on how to use it
- Telephone support, to provide on-going advice

In addition, they intend to assemble a database of best and worst practice, a website, tailored training programmes and consultancy support designed to meet client needs.

The use of the internet to disseminate good practice and practical advice will also be essential to improve the knowledge base of professionals. Use of CD-ROMs, video conferencing and IT networks will play an increasingly important role in skills and knowledge development, as well as in the day to day working lives of professionals.

Sustaining communities course in Cornwall

Penwith HA in Cornwall has embarked on a long-term strategy to better equip its housing staff to work with communities in regeneration activity. It has set up a Sustaining Communities course in conjunction with Cornwall College and the CIH. Its housing officers will gain accreditation through open-learning over the course of a year or so by acquiring skills in facilitating and assisting the communities in which they work, in a pragmatic way. This is designed to avoid communities feeling they are being taken over by the professionals.

The RSL set up a specialist Social Investment Unit in September 1999 in order to acquire the necessary skills and resources to become more involved in neighbourhood regeneration initiatives. It is also undergoing a thorough review of its customer services and management of regeneration initiatives, to provide better linkages between its specialist unit and its other housing professionals delivering mainstream services.

In addition, the main training organisations will be developing more individually focused training, personal development events and programmes. Training organisations such as the Chartered Institute of Housing (CIH) are developing programmes to equip individuals with the necessary skills and approaches.

❏ Sources of advice, support and guidance

The present range of training providers or organisations promoting training needs includes:

- Universities and colleges
- Professional bodies
- Umbrella organisations and trade bodies
- Charitable bodies
- Private consultancies

The main providers are all adapting their programmes to the new requirements of neighbourhood renewal and Neighbourhood Management.

■ Chartered Institute of Housing (CIH)

As the principal body for setting and accrediting professional housing management standards, the CIH has a keen interest in making sure the skills and knowledge base of housing professionals is adequate to meet the new Neighbourhood Management agenda. They are tailoring their professional qualifications, training and seminar programmes to better equip staff with the skills they need. This will be an evolving picture as experience in Neighbourhood Management and awareness of the skills required develops. The following initiatives are some of those currently in the pipeline:

- A new core component on inter-agency working within the professional qualification, the degree level qualification which is the primary professional standard for housing management staff. It is now a core requirement on the majority of certificate courses undertaken through further education colleges and through distance learning with the CIH
- Recent development of a new course leading to a National Certificate in Housing: Sustainable Communities, which is delivered through the CIH's own Distance Learning Centre; this accompanies an existing certificate course for caretaking and concierge staff.
- A social exclusion and regeneration conference in 2001 and further joint seminars with the Social Exclusion Unit (SEU) and the National Housing Federation (NHF)

- The development of courses and an education programme, which will enable housing professionals to qualify as neighbourhood managers
- The development of courses on capacity building, training and inter-agency networking
- Leicester University is developing a course which will be accredited by the CIH – it is a masters degree in the management of partnership and collaboration and will be open to senior housing personnel

■ National Housing Federation

As the main trade body for RSLs, the NHF has lobbied hard for social housing providers to be substantially involved in shaping and delivering the neighbourhood regeneration strategy and Neighbourhood Management.

It is involved in the inter-agency Neighbourhood Renewal Network, which is keen to ensure the development of appropriate skills and knowledge for housing professionals.

It will be ensuring that its member organisations are kept informed about issues and policies as they emerge. A development and regeneration conference will focus heavily on sharing knowledge and good practice on a number of regeneration topics, including Neighbourhood Management, communication skills and networking.

■ Others

The Housing Corporation

The Housing Corporation has a new regulatory approach consisting of lead regulators, inspectors and financial appraisal teams. The lead regulator will have an on-going relationship with RSLs with over 250 homes and will agree the regulatory plan as well as the financial analysis from the financial appraisal team. The inspectors will therefore test the service on the ground by talking to tenants and other stakeholders. The new regulatory approach will be outcome focused and will use as a basis for evaluation the Regulatory Code and guidance.

Housing Potential UK (HPUK)

This is the National Training Organisation promoting training needs for the housing sector, sponsored by the CIH, NHF and the Local Government Association (LGA).

With Department for Education and Skills funding it has carried out an extensive skills audit of the housing sector to develop a workforce training and development plan. It has recognised the need for skills training in community development and regeneration work.

Neighbourhood Renewal Unit (NRU)

The Government has set up the NRU to provide leadership and an overview on Neighbourhood Management, located within the DTLR.

Within the NRU a Skills and Knowledge team will be set up to establish a learning and development strategy, which will:

- Embed a focus on learning and development at all levels of the National Strategy for Neighbourhood Renewal
- Identify gaps and weaknesses in current learning provision and, where necessary, commission practical training packages
- Look at how learning and development can be funded for those with limited financial resources
- Consider whether changes need to be made to occupational standards in order to equip public sector professionals with the skills they need to play a more effective part in neighbourhood renewal
- Consider where joint learning is appropriate and how to promote it
- Examine the role for Government Offices in auditing and tailoring learning and development opportunities to meet regional needs, drawing on available expertise and innovation

The other significant role for the Skills and Knowledge team will be the introduction of a knowledge management system. This is intended to be a comprehensive system to collect and disseminate good practice within deprived neighbourhoods. It will involve a national website and opportunities for one to one advice (see Chapter 8).

Investors in Communities (IiC) is an accreditation scheme for residents' organisations and RSLs working together to tackle social exclusion. It will act as a clearing house for ideas and experience and help to establish common standards. A two year pilot programme was announced in May 2001.

IiC has the support of the National Housing Federation and has been developed by Hastoe Housing Association. The DTLR, the Housing Corporation, the Countryside Agency and the Joseph Rowntree Foundation have contributed £400,000 to fund the pilot.

The Housing Corporation, the **DTLR** and the **SEU** are all providing substantial information and advice through their websites and in published guidance notes, reports and circulars.

TPAS (England) also provides a telephone helpline service to tenants in England.

CHAPTER 7

IMPLEMENTING
NEIGHBOURHOOD MANAGEMENT

What this Chapter is about

This chapter sets out some practical guidelines on how to implement
Neighbourhood Management, including:

- How to get started
- Establishing the right delivery vehicles
- Assembling a locally based team
- Developing a neighbourhood action plan
- Establishing neighbourhood agreements

*'If Neighbourhood Management is to make a difference where other initiatives have
failed, everyone, from communities to local authorities – needs to be convinced,
firstly, that it is different from what has gone before, and secondly, that it is worth
the considerable energies and costs that will be involved. Bringing excluded areas in
from the cold will mean getting rid of old ways of doing things and taking risks. It is
unlikely to be a comfortable ride.'*

Source: Taylor, M (2000)

Most stakeholders will not be starting from scratch with Neighbourhood
Management; local authorities and RSLs are used to running area-based
projects and initiatives, often with a degree of delegation to locally-based teams.
A housing management service has traditionally been delivered in many areas
on a neighbourhood basis by local authorities, but less so by RSLs with their
often more dispersed stock.

Neighbourhood Management poses a substantial challenge, not least because it
is a long-term process, not a time limited, ring-fenced budgeted project or
initiative, but also because it challenges many of the ways in which services
have traditionally been delivered.

To add to the complications, most services in an area are not delivered at neighbourhood level, but often across whole boroughs. Many specialist services are targeted at individuals, not communities. The contract culture in the public sector means that neighbourhood managers will need to have a place at the contract negotiation stage if many services are to be influenced. Targeting neighbourhoods and disassembling budgets is likely to have cost implications for delivery.

There is, however, no model for Neighbourhood Management. The process is very much in its infancy but, to be successful, it needs to be tailored closely to local circumstances. What is right in one neighbourhood will not work in another. Much of this has to do with the nature of local communities and their capacity and interest in being involved. Community involvement, in whatever form, is certainly a pre-requisite for every stage of the following framework.

How to get started

By:
- Identifying the appropriate areas
- Identifying the natural leaders
- Getting the right information
- Identifying the financial resources
- Establishing a delivery vehicle
- Assembling a neighbourhood-based staff team
- Drawing up a Neighbourhood Action Plan
- Disaggregating budgets to neighbourhood level
- Establishing neighbourhood agreements with service providers
- Carrots and sticks
- Linking to other initiatives and strategies

❑ Identifying the appropriate areas

Neighbourhoods can be defined in different ways – by political wards, existing service boundaries, physical barriers, consistency of tenure and design, catchment areas for essential services or by areas which local residents themselves identify as their patch. Most research suggests that neighbourhood approaches work best in small, relatively homogenous areas, which residents themselves relate to.

The Government's guidance to Neighbourhood Management pathfinders on identifying suitable areas stressed the following key factors:

- Bringing local groups and bodies together within the 83 eligible areas to decide which neighbourhood should be prioritised

- Focusing on areas where there is a real need for change, but not necessarily the most deprived
- Areas which are large enough to enable services to be co-ordinated and delivered effectively, but small enough to be responsive to community needs and priorities. In practice, this means between 2,500 and 5,000 households
- Areas which already have a strong community base which can respond quickly to early action, rather than those needing extensive capacity building
- A wide diversity of neighbourhoods, to test the principles of Neighbourhood Management in different contexts

The best areas to begin Neighbourhood Management are therefore likely to be reasonably cohesive, identifiable neighbourhoods, with communities already keen to see change and make it happen.

The focus on neighbourhoods of around 4-5,000 households and 15,000 people is understandable in national strategic terms. But there is a good case for testing out Neighbourhood Management in smaller areas – around 1,000 homes. There is already some evidence that smaller areas can take on aspects of Neighbourhood Management and make it work and there is no doubt that communities see their own neighbourhoods as often quite tightly defined – sometimes no more than a few streets. This is likely to be particularly the case on single ownership estates and in rural areas.

In inner cities and larger estates, however, communities may see their neighbourhoods in larger terms. A two tier form of Neighbourhood Management, with the wider area dealing with service delivery and smaller sub-neighbourhoods dealing with other community priorities, may be more appropriate here.

Neighbourhood service pilots in Liverpool

There are six neighbourhood services pilots in Liverpool, run by the City Council. The areas selected had no history of recent investment, contained a mix of tenures and comprised 500-1000 homes each.

Netherley was one of the smallest pilot areas and was originally an owner occupied peripheral estate of 600 homes. Residents had big issues around environmental services – youth gatherings, car theft, vandalism, intimidation, poor quality roads, chewed up open space, poor street and path lighting. Netherley ranks 43rd of 8414 wards in the Local Index of Deprivation.

Key factors in choosing the pilot locations included:

- Do public sector services meet residents' aspirations?
- Should the City Council change the way service pilots are delivered?
- Can the community be effectively engaged?

Neighbourhood Services was set up by the City Council in late 1999 with a group of part time co-ordinators, seconded from various public and private sector agencies. In June 2000, they became full time and each took the lead on one pilot.

To fall into line with the National Strategy, each neighbourhood was increased to 4,000-5,000 houses. This created some resistance from the communities, who felt they might lose out if other neighbourhoods were included in theirs.

The expanded neighbourhoods were defined by ward boundaries – this fitted community perceptions of boundaries in some areas, but in others it was more problematic.

❑ Identifying the natural leaders

Deciding who leads the Neighbourhood Management process is a crucial early decision once the target area has been selected. The main factors in reaching a decision are likely to be:

1. Who wants to do it?
2. Who has the largest stake?
3. Who has the most clout?
4. Who works best with the local community?
5. Who works best with the local authority and other public service providers?
6. How strong is the local community?
7. Is there a potential delivery vehicle already established?

The answers to these questions may well throw up several potential leaders. Local authorities, RSLs, voluntary and community sector agencies, private sector companies and not least local communities themselves are all potential leaders of the Neighbourhood Management process. Much will depend on local circumstances. Where there is a choice, local communities themselves should be centrally involved in making it.

There is a clear process by which housing organisations, and particularly RSLs, can get involved in Neighbourhood Management – through the renewal of existing areas where they have a substantial stake. In some places, local authorities may be best placed to take a lead role, but not in all. Having the local assets should not mean that RSLs or local authorities automatically become the lead agent on Neighbourhood Management. Both may be better placed to play a supportive and enabling role.

In some neighbourhoods, it may be appropriate to set up a completely new delivery vehicle for Neighbourhood Management, in consultation with the local community.

Local authorities and RSLs also need to be careful about how they get into Neighbourhood Management – it needs discreet skills. Well thought out, evolutionary strategies are needed, not knee jerk reactions and chasing funding. Neighbourhood Management is about managing neighbourhoods, not increasing asset size.

In some neighbourhoods, local communities will want to take the lead themselves and the role of RSLs and local authorities should be to facilitate this process. Chapter 4 includes some useful case studies on how this can be successfully achieved.

Dingle Housing Regeneration Company
CDS Housing, Liverpool

CDS Housing has set up a new Regeneration Company called INCLUDE, a non-charitable subsidiary of the Association. It is intended that this subsidiary becomes a stock-holding RSL and registration with the Housing Corporation is expected by summer 2001.

The Company will have two broad objectives:

- Community regeneration programmes for the area
- Physical improvements to the housing stock and environment

INCLUDE will become a property owner and landlord and will become the designated stock transfer body for Liverpool City Council (LCC), CDS and other RSLs. Other physical, non-housing assets are also intended to be owned by the company.

It will provide on-the-spot Neighbourhood Management, using local Public Service Agreements with LCC and other links with service providers such as schools. Residents will be given direct control and involvement in service quality and effectiveness and opportunities to run services themselves. The local community and other stakeholders will be closely involved in drawing up the priorities and workplan for the new company.

The long-term aim is to regenerate the area through an integrated approach to physical, economic and social regeneration. It will identify land and buildings that require direct action to improve the neighbourhood, through redevelopment and environmental maintenance. INCLUDE sees one of its priorities as being to provide leadership to and joining up of existing services and funding streams.

INCLUDE is seen by LCC as the natural home for any pilot initiative in developing locally managed services. LCC is currently considering devolving its environmental maintenance budget (which includes street sweeping, dumped rubbish removal, vacant land treatment etc). INCLUDE would act as the contractor for the City Council.

❑ Getting the right information

Neighbourhoods cannot be managed unless those doing it have information on what services are provided, by whom, on what basis and at what cost. Much of this information, particularly on costs and budgets, is often unavailable at neighbourhood level. A great deal of work is needed to pull it all together. Agencies need to work closely together to collect and co-ordinate this information in the early stages of any Neighbourhood Management initiative. Without it, decisions about future changes will be constrained.

Some local authorities have already developed area co-ordination systems which enable this information to be collected and used to start the process of devolving service responsibilities and delivery down to local level. The New Deal for Communities programmes are required by Government to make assessments of total public expenditure within their neighbourhoods, as part of their baseline assessments.

The Government is committed to developing neighbourhood statistics, with ward level information available during 2001 and Census information in 2003. This should enable local communities and their partners to pinpoint neighbourhood problems and target solutions more effectively.

Mainstream spending in East Brighton

Total public expenditure in the East Brighton NDC area in 1998/99

Services	£
Policing	642,000
Probation	200,000
Health Authority	10,938,000
South Downs Health NHS Trust	3,012,400
Council Services	36,916,200
Sub total	**51,708,600**
Benefits	
Housing Benefit/Council Tax rebate	17,170,850
Jobseekers Allowance	2,006,160
Income Support	7,119,840
Sub total	**26,296,850**
Total Services and Benefits	**78,005,450**
Average per household (5,594)	14,123
Average per individual (15,564)	5,076

Source: Abstracted from East Brighton NDC Delivery Plan (2000)

Finding out what services are provided and how much is spent on them is the first stage of a comprehensive neighbourhood service audit – a key stage in collecting baseline information to inform the Neighbourhood Action Plan which will follow.

This audit needs to look at the following for each service provider:

- Budgeted neighbourhood expenditure
- Staff resources deployed directly at neighbourhood level
- An estimate of the proportion of central staff resources and other overheads which should be accounted for at neighbourhood level
- Neighbourhood offices and related equipment and assets
- Any forward commitments in terms of service contracts, service level agreements

Getting hold of this information will not usually be easy. Some of it may require negotiation, rather than simple extraction of existing information. It may not therefore be possible to assemble all of it at the start of the Neighbourhood Management process. There is much to be said for starting with the service providers who are already signed up to the Neighbourhood Management approach and tackling those that are not at a later stage.

The information requirements are not just quantitative. The quality of services, how they are perceived by residents and the impact they have on their communities are all equally, if not more important.

Every neighbourhood will have different priorities, but the main priorities for most residents are likely to centre around some or all of the following:

- The availability of information on local services
- How services are currently co-ordinated
- How quickly service providers respond to local problems
- How local people can have a direct say in service provision
- How local jobs can be created and sustained in local services

Finding out how residents view local service provision is therefore vital (see Chapter 4 – Consultation and Involvement). There are many well-established techniques for doing so, including:

- Community planning and visioning
- Planning for Real
- Citizens' Juries
- Traditional surveys and questionnaires
- Roadshows and focus groups

The first two techniques take time to set up and deliver and usually form part of a broader community capacity building process (see Chapter 5). They have the advantage of enabling a community to develop an informed opinion over time. Neighbourhood Management priorities can develop as an integral part of a more broadly based community plan in which residents articulate their priorities for change and put forward realistic proposals for achieving it. The last two techniques can provide useful snapshots on local perceptions at a particular point in time.

Regular walkabouts with residents and service providers can also play an important role in finding out what actually happens in a neighbourhood day to day – something which service provider managers see only occasionally.

What residents think about services in East Brighton

- There is a lack of confidence in the ability of the Police to bring wrong-doers to justice. The Council is criticised for failing to enforce tenancy conditions. In particular, residents resent the Council's failure to take action against drug dealers
- Lack of information and difficulties in making contact with support services is seen as a fundamental problem, as is the perceived mistrust of service providers, and feelings that service provision simply does not match the real needs of people
- There are barriers and misunderstandings between residents and the 'people in suits' (statutory agency workers). This is an issue of widespread concern relating to all public services
- The cost, frequency and routing of local bus services all make it more difficult to get to work, find a job, and make use of services and amenities that are mostly located in the town centre
- Both the Employment Service and Benefits Agency need to be more sympathetic and sensitive to the needs of new entrants to the labour market, and less judgemental about people who find it difficult to sustain long-term employment because of family commitments or lack of appropriate skills and experience.
- Residents feel that too many changes made in the past have been imposed on them without sufficient consultation and have not reflected their needs
- There is widespread criticism of the Council's repair services
- Residents feel that there is poor access to appropriate primary care services in East Brighton and complain about the lack of alternatives to prescription drugs

Source: Abstracted from the East Brighton NDC Delivery Plan (2000)

A further example of successful information gathering processes can be found in East London:

Community Planning, Poplar HARCA, London

The Teviot Estate is located in the London Borough of Tower Hamlets. It is an estate of mainly low rise public housing and one of seven neighbourhoods where Poplar HARCA, a local housing company, is leading the community regeneration and Neighbourhood Management process. Residents in each neighbourhood have produced their own Community Plan. This is how Teviot developed theirs:

- Grumble walks were held in spring 1999, where residents walked around the estate identifying problem areas and proposing some solutions
- An away day was held that included local agency members and residents where a draft vision, aims and objectives for the Plan were agreed
- A Poplar HARCA Estate Board meeting was followed by an Estate Board open meeting in November 1999 where a skeleton plan was agreed. Also in November local agencies agreed the skeleton plan. They held discussion groups with their users to ensure their views were fed into what would be the final Community Action Plan
- In May 2000 a Planning for Real exercise was held, to ensure that as many residents as possible were consulted on priorities for action within the Community Action Plan. This involved the local primary school building a scale model of the Plan during which time they were consulted on their priorities for action. This model was then the centrepiece of a Community Action Plan fun day attended by over 300 residents
- After the fun day a prioritising workshop was held to help inform a timetable for action, which was based on the views of those present at the prioritising workshop and residents requesting specific action
- Presentation of the final drafts of the Teviot Community Action Plan to the August meetings of both the Teviot Estate Board and to local agencies for final amendments
- The completed Teviot Community Action Plan was then presented to the Poplar HARCA Board and the London Borough of Tower Hamlets for comment and, where relevant, action in September 2000. It was printed and bound and distributed to all residents of the Teviot estate and all relevant organisations. It is now being implemented

Source: Abstracted from the Teviot Community Plan 2000

❏ Identifying the financial resources

Setting up and running Neighbourhood Management is likely to be resource intensive initially, something recognised by Government in its proposals for pathfinder funding. However, as the new way of delivering services beds down and more is learned about what works, there is an expectation that re-allocating and bending existing budgets should be sufficient to cover costs. Indeed Neighbourhood Management is unlikely to be sustainable if it requires a continual injection of 'special project' funding once up and running. Identifying what resources are already in existence in an area and other areas is therefore essential (see Chapters 3 and 4).

Neighbourhood Management in a typical area of 4,500-5,000 households is expected to cost around £300,000 a year. The PAT4 report provided the following breakdown, upon which the pathfinder guidance is based:

Typical Neighbourhood Management costs
4,500-5,000 households

Function	Cost
Neighbourhood manager	£50,000
Administration/PA	£18,000
Community support manager	£30,000
Admin/Organiser	£16,000
On-costs @ 20%	£34,800
Materials and equipment	£45,000
Office costs	£25,000
Community Fund (£20 per household per year)	£90,000
Total	**£308,800**

Source: Social Exclusion Unit (2000a)

These costs do not include specific Neighbourhood Management projects, such as neighbourhood wardens and Environmental Task Forces, both of which would require additional funding.

The likely costs of setting up Neighbourhood Management in smaller areas, say around 1000 homes, are set out below:

Typical Neighbourhood Management costs
1000 households

Function	Cost
Neighbourhood manager	£35,000
Administrative/community support	£16,000
On-costs @ 20%	£10,200
Materials and equipment	£10,000
Office costs	£5,000
Community Fund (£20 per household per year)	£20,000
Community support manager (50% of costs)	£15,000
Total	**£111,200**

Source: Social Exclusion Unit (2000a)

In the Neighbourhood Management pathfinder and New Deal for Communities areas, the Government is providing a substantial funding package.

A maximum seven year funding package is available from Government Offices for the two year pilot programme of 30 Neighbourhood Management initiatives, including:

- Up to **£200,000** management and administrative costs to develop the Neighbourhood Management strategy and build community engagement
- Up to **£200,000** to meet the partnership's ongoing management and administration costs and the set up costs for a Neighbourhood Management team
- Around **£300,000** a year, reducing to zero by year seven, in a project and leverage fund.

Outside these areas, no special funding is currently earmarked specifically for Neighbourhood Management. Potential funding sources for piloting Neighbourhood Management here are likely to include:

Potential funding sources
Non-pathfinder and NDC areas

- Neighbourhood Renewal Fund
- Existing SRB5 and 6 programmes
- RSL housing management and other revenue budgets
- Local authority service budgets, including housing
- Other statutory agencies; i.e. Police, Health Trusts etc
- Housing Corporation Innovation and Good Practice Grants
- Private finance initiatives

❑ Establishing a delivery vehicle

The successful delivery of Neighbourhood Management will depend heavily on having in place a locally-accountable body with responsibility for overseeing the process and to whom the Neighbourhood Management team will report. There is no one model; neighbourhoods should be encouraged to develop their own vehicles. In some cases, existing bodies might usefully be adapted, or their brief expanded, to take on the Neighbourhood Management role. In other areas, setting up Neighbourhood Service Panels may be a useful stepping stone to more permanent arrangements. Much will depend on what is currently on the ground, who has taken the lead and particularly the strength of the local community at the outset.

If they are to have strong community involvement, delivery vehicles will take time to set up and even longer to bed themselves in. Professionals need to work at the resident's pace, not their own. Starting with something modest, with an objective of taking on much more later on, has much to commend it.

The need for time

It has taken two to three years for Highland to disaggregate service budgets onto an areas basis and then devolve budgets to 500 budget holders...

The Tipton Challenge Partnership needed three to four years of community development before it went live...

The Royds Community Association worked for three years with a local authority housing officer and a private sector individual before they submitted their successful SRB bid...the Bloomsbury Estate Management Board is now in its ninth year and still developing.

Source: Taylor M (2000)

Meetings and paperwork need to be resident, not agency oriented. Replication of old SRB Partnerships, often dominated by professionals with only modest resident involvement will not do. A more radical approach is needed, which draws residents and professionals together in a genuine, not a superficial, partnership.

Potential vehicles for delivering Neighbourhood Management include (see Chapter 4 for more details):
- Service improvement panels
- Community associations
- Estate management boards
- Tenant management co-operatives
- Community based housing associations and co-ops
- Local housing companies
- Neighbourhood boards
- Neighbourhood trusts
- Community development trusts
- Village companies
- Resident service organisations

The strong emphasis on community leadership and the need for workable partnerships with service providers suggests that, whatever the vehicle for delivery, the key objectives should be as follows:

1. **Constitutions and powers**
   - A body which is able to provide community ownership of the process and accountability for its decisions
   - A body which is flexible enough to incorporate informal processes, such as networking, to achieve its objectives
   - A body which has the powers it needs to oversee service delivery and/or deliver local services itself

2. **Representation**
   - A body which has substantial resident representation and preferably an inbuilt resident majority on its main Board and Executive Committee
   - A body which is chaired by an elected local resident or someone in whom local residents have confidence
   - A body which includes senior nominees of all the main service providers involved in the Neighbourhood Management process

3. **Local democracy**
   - A body which holds annual neighbourhood elections for its resident members
   - A body which actively seeks to include often excluded groups, such as young people, in its management arrangements
   - A body which encourages discussion and decision making through informal as well as formal meetings, to build consensus and help resolve conflicts

4. **Training and support**
   - A body which provides regular, on-going training and support for all its Board members
   - A body which seeks to recompense its resident members for their voluntary input (there are benefit and tax complications to be resolved here)

An example of a delivery vehicle may be:

The Firthmoor Community Partnership Board, Darlington

The Partnership Board is responsible for an estate based SRB6 programme, with a specific focus on Neighbourhood Management.

The 17 strong Board comprises nine community representatives and eight nominees from partner agencies, including three from the local authority. The chair is a resident. All the resident Board members are elected annually through estate elections. Three places on the Board are reserved for Darlington Borough Council nominees. No decisions can be made unless there is a majority of residents present at a Board meeting.

A further example:

• •

Royds Community Association Board, Bradford

The community association leads a major £30 million SRB programme covering three estates and acts as its own accountable body. The Board comprises 22 directors, 12 of them locally elected residents. Most of its committees and groups are chaired by local people.

An extensive programme of support and training is provided for Board members, and around £400,000 a year is spent on community capacity building, partly to enable the local communities to be centrally involved at all levels of the organisation.

Around 400 resident volunteers are involved in a wide variety of activities on the estates.

• •

Sectors represented on the delivery vehicle might include some or all of the following, depending on the neighbourhood:

Sectors and groups which might be represented on delivery vehicles

- Benefits Agency
- Communities of interest
- Community organisations
- Employment Service/New Deal Partnerships
- Faith communities
- Further education colleges
- Health Authorities/Primary Care Groups and Trusts
- Local authorities
- Local councillors
- Police forces/Police Authority/Fire Service
- Private businesses
- RSLs
- Residents
- Schools
- Voluntary organisations

Source: Adapted from the Social Exclusion Unit National Strategy Action Plan (2001b)

❑ Assembling a neighbourhood based staff team

Bringing a team of people together to deliver Neighbourhood Management is a major challenge. In many areas, this will involve the appointment or secondment of professionals, working within an agreed structure and reporting to some form of community-led neighbourhood board.

The following factors are likely to be important when agencies and communities are deciding how to assemble an appropriate team:

- Neighbourhood Management is new and residents' expectations of it are likely to be high. There may be a perception that if new neighbourhood staff are simply the same people who have been working in the area for years, but with a make-over that things may not change.

  However with support and a willingness to adapt to this new and differing area of work and in consultation with the community, neighbourhood housing managers may be potential candidates for this role.

- Neighbourhood managers need specific qualities which are relatively rare in many service organisations. They must act independently of major providers, but be able to influence them at the highest levels; they must be able to broker deals one day and thump the table of service directors the next; and they must build confidence and respect amongst the local community. Experience and status with both senior professionals and residents is important. It is likely to prove a tricky balancing act.

  Casting the net widely when advertising, i.e. beyond the housing and regeneration weeklies, is likely to be beneficial in attracting these sort of candidates.

- Neighbourhood Management teams will inevitably vary in both scale and scope. In some neighbourhoods it may make sense to bring into the team a number of seconded agency staff with a neighbourhood brief; in others, a manager and support staff may be more appropriate and all that is required. Neighbourhood Management should certainly not be an opportunity for empire building.

- Salaries for key staff, particularly the Neighbourhood Manager, must be pitched at a level which will attract people with the vision, commitment and shrewdness to make the process a success. £35,000 – £60,000 a year is a sensible target range.

- Community based offices are essential – Neighbourhood Management is not something which can be done at a distance. The use of existing local authority or RSL neighbourhood offices should generally be avoided. Basing the new team in an existing community-run centre, a converted house or even a portacabin is preferable – it makes a clean break with the past.

Summary person specifications and job descriptions from two areas leading the Neighbourhood Management process are set out in the following charts.

....

A typical Job Description for a Neighbourhood Manager

Main purpose of the job

1. Overall accountability to the Neighbourhood Board for improving and joining up local services and making them more responsive to local needs.

2. Responsibility for ensuring that the Neighbourhood Board is supported and properly advised, and that their decisions are effectively implemented.

Key responsibilities

1. Supporting the Neighbourhood Board, acting as lead officer, supporting the chair and acting as the neighbourhood's advocate on behalf of the Board.

2. Improving local services, through monitoring service delivery, measuring service performance, developing new projects and negotiating service level agreements.

3. Developing, implementing and reviewing the Annual Neighbourhood Plan.

4. Project Management.

5. Partnership working, providing the main point of contact for services, promoting collaborative working relationships and developing integrated plans and strategies for the neighbourhood.

6. Community involvement, through promoting widespread involvement in the process, supporting capacity building and ensuring inclusive representation.

7. Management of the staff team, reviewing organisational structures and operations and developing appropriate quality accreditation.

8. Financial management, through compliance with budgetary and financial good practice, formulating and monitoring annual budgets and reporting to the Board.

9. Promoting the neighbourhood's potential, involving political representatives in the process and complying with equal opportunities good practice.

Source: Abstracted and summarised from the East Brighton NDC programme, (2000)

....

A typical Person Specification for a Neighbourhood Manager

ATTRIBUTES   **JOB REQUIREMENTS**

KNOWLEDGE   An understanding of the following areas is important, but direct work experience is not necessarily required.
- Local Government and other public services
- Private, voluntary and community sector organisations
- Characteristics and needs of areas of multiple deprivation
- Policy and legislation on social and urban regeneration
- Community development and involvement policy and practice

SKILLS AND ABILITIES   A multi-skilled person who can operate effectively in situations of multiple accountability and exercise influence without traditional line management authority.
- Project management
- Knowing 'what works' in community regeneration
- Enabling and empowering communities
- Team building
- Leadership
- Problem solving, conflict resolution, brokerage
- Negotiating and influencing
- Political shrewdness
- Excellent written and verbal communication skills
- Community and customer approach to service delivery
- Strategic planning
- Ability to deliver programme to deadlines/budgets
- Financial management
- Monitoring and evaluation
- Understanding diversity
- Risk management
- Networking
- Learning from others

EXPERIENCE
- People and project management at a senior level
- Effective operation across organisational boundaries gained in the public, private or community/voluntary sectors
- Working directly with communities in areas of multiple deprivation
- Understanding of and commitment to equal opportunities policy and practice

Source: Abstracted from the Firthmoor Community Works SRB6 programme, (2000)

❑ Drawing up a Neighbourhood Action Plan

The Neighbourhood Action Plan should be an annually reviewed public document, written in plain English and translated where appropriate. It should be negotiated and agreed with the neighbourhood delivery body and, as a pre-requisite, it should have widespread community support. A summary document should be circulated to every household.

It will inevitably take some time to put together, 6-12 months after the start of the Neighbourhood Management process is probably a sensible target.

The Neighbourhood Action Plan should:

- Set out the **long term vision**, three year strategy, year one plan and immediate priorities, with appropriate milestones, outputs and performance targets

- Set out the **key objectives** of the Neighbourhood Management process, the delivery arrangements and local staffing

- Provide comprehensive and up-to-date **baseline information for residents** on how local services are provided, who provides them and how much they cost

- Be clear about **what can and cannot be influenced** by the Action Plan. Be specific about which services will not be included in the Neighbourhood Management arrangements as well as those that will, and explain why

- Prioritise services and providers which can be influenced **now** and which can make a significant difference to people's lives

- Highlight **'quick win'** activities, which will help to convince sceptical residents that Neighbourhood Management can make an impact

- Set up **resident hotlines** or other mechanisms which deliver quick response times to people's complaints or suggestions

- Explain **how residents can get involved** in the Neighbourhood Management arrangements

- Explain **how the Action Plan will be reviewed** and the effectiveness of the Neighbourhood Management arrangements evaluated in the future

An example of draft milestones is as follows:

Firthmoor Community Works, Darlington

Neighbourhood Management
Draft milestones

Appointment of Neighbourhood Manager	**January 2001**
Formal secondment of NM Team	**April 2001**
Agree NM objectives with Community Partnership and key partners	**May 2001**
Agree NM performance indicators for service delivery with Community Partnership and key partners	**May 2001**
2001/2002 Annual Plan agreed with Community Partnership	**July 2001**
Evaluation arrangements in place	**September 2001**
Seminar for key NM partners	**October 2001**
2002/2003 Annual Plan agreed with Community Partnership	**March 2002**
Relocate team to new Community Centre	**July 2002**
Review of NM arrangements and service co-ordination	**March 2003**
Formal external evaluation of NM arrangements	**February 2004**
Transfer of NM funding to local authority	**April 2005**

The Year One Action Plan needs to be realistic – changing the way services are delivered in neighbourhoods is a long term process. It will not happen overnight. It will take time to bring some service providers on board. Not all the budgetary information will be available from day one. Beginning modest and practical rather than ambitious and radical is probably a sensible maxim in the first year.

Neighbourhood Action Plans have a potentially wider scope than managing local services. Residents' priorities may include, amongst other things, development opportunities, demolition of low demand properties, re-establishing neighbourhood shops or creating local jobs. Action Plans need to look beyond services and address the whole neighbourhood agenda. They may, for example, make proposals for the creation of community-owned assets. Some may go further and include proposals for neighbourhood development frameworks, creating new operational guidelines for social, economic and physical development specific to individual neighbourhoods.

❑ Disaggregating budgets to neighbourhood level

Disaggregating the budgets of service providers down to neighbourhood level is likely to prove one of the most difficult tasks in the Neighbourhood Action Plan. Early decisions will be needed on what can realistically be ring-fenced at neighbourhood level, what is negotiable and what is not and whether budget pooling between service providers can be achieved. (see Chapter 5).

Much will depend on the willingness of service providers who are signed-up to the Neighbourhood Management approach to use some of their internal resources to disaggregate their budgets. Once done, the sensitive task of deciding which parts of these budgets can be placed under local control, through the neighbourhood delivery vehicle, can then begin. This is unlikely to be either a quick or easy process and will almost certainly require a lengthy period of negotiation.

How much control over service budgets is eventually devolved to neighbourhood level will depend on the determination of service providers to overcome the many obstacles involved and the pressure placed on them to do so by local communities. Tenant management organisations have demonstrated that the task is not impossible, but the different rules for different services, the lack of any direct relationship between them and provider fears about non-devolved services and their budgets, may inhibit substantial early progress.

The options, ranked from nominal to radical, are likely to include:

Options for budget devolution to neighbourhoods

- Monitoring 'shadow' budgets
- Control over small budgets
- Control over revenue budgets within financial regulations
- Control over specific service budgets
- Flexible virement rules for revenue budgets
- Flexible rules for carrying forward surpluses
- Freedom to purchase certain services direct
- Control over staffing structures and salary gradings
- Freedom to raise additional revenues through service charges
- Freedom to raise additional capital

Source: Hambleton et al (1997)

For example:

Towards local control of service budgets
Poplar HARCA, London

The HARCA's six tenant-run Estate Boards are enabling local residents to build up knowledge and experience to challenge and influence key decisions about all local services and priorities, not just those provided by the HARCA. The next steps towards local control of service delivery are:

- Routine services will be accessible through a central Customer Services Team based at the heart of Poplar and providing assistance to personal, telephone and email enquiries in the main community languages
- Key services provided by Poplar HARCA will be devolved to the local level
- The focus for estate level services, from whatever agency, will be Poplar HARCA's neighbourhood officers. Each one will be based on-the-spot, dealing with the more complex housing management issues across the **estate** and linking up with other agencies where support and /or action is required
- Co-ordination at a **neighbourhood** level will be provided by a neighbourhood services manager who will supervise the delivery of services provided in-house, by co-located agencies and through service level agreements
- The policy and priority framework will be determined by a neighbourhood manager in conjunction with the neighbourhood partnership board

❑ Establishing neighbourhood agreements with service providers

With a Neighbourhood Action Plan in place and neighbourhood budgets negotiated, formal agreements will need to be brokered between local communities and service providers. Recent experience in this field is limited but growing; a number of local authority housing departments and RSLs have been involved in developing estate agreements. Neighbourhood managers will need to be aware of specific issues relating to work with non-unitary local authorities when discussing such agreements. Recent research into 19 of these, by Ian Cole et al (*Neighbourhood Agreements in Action*, JRF, 2000) has provided important pointers for Neighbourhood Management arrangements.

The essence of estate or neighbourhood agreements is to provide a vehicle for formal arrangements between residents and those responsible for delivering local services. Such agreements may cover a number of aspects, including the following:

- Service standards
- Response times
- Targets
- Budgets

Most of those already up and running have a predominantly housing and estate service focus; they have not yet involved other neighbourhood services or taken a wider neighbourhood perspective. Broadwater Farm in Haringey is one of the exceptions. Here, residents had demanded that their agreement should go beyond housing to cover issues such as childcare, jobs and training, crime and drug-related problems.

On large council estates there may initially be an overlap between Tenant Participation Compacts and neighbourhood agreements. As Neighbourhood Management beds down, however, it may be sensible to incorporate the former into the latter.

In those neighbourhoods with a mix of housing tenures, neighbourhood agreements provide an opportunity to achieve a consistency of service amongst different landlords, as well as developing partnerships between them and other service providers.

Setting up a neighbourhood agreement takes time – a large element of community capacity building is likely to be involved, particularly in neighbourhoods where the community infrastructure is not yet strong. The setting up process will vary between neighbourhoods, but in most cases it is likely to include:

- Determining residents' priorities
- Agreeing which services should be included in the agreement
- Defining providers' roles and responsibilities
- Reviewing existing contractual arrangements
- Negotiating service level agreements
- Setting realistic targets
- Agreeing monitoring arrangements
- Preparing a formal document

Local authorities and RSLs are in a good position to facilitate the development of neighbourhood agreements – indeed, it is difficult to see how they will develop more widely unless landlords are directly involved. But they need to be resident, not agency-driven agreements.

The research by Ian Cole et al suggests that sustainability is likely to be a key issue for many agreements. They need to be developed as constructive and dynamic responses to local problems and concerns, rather than as a 'once and for all' statement that could eventually fall into disuse.

Foxwood Estate Agreement, York

The Foxwood Neighbourhood Agreement began life as a community safety and crime initiative on a mixed council and registered social landlord estate of 1362 homes. The Foxwood Community Action Group manages the agreement and deals directly with service providers, following a programme of training and support from a community development worker. The agreement has had a major impact on estate residents and service providers. It has:

- Successfully facilitated inter-agency working
- Empowered local residents involved in the Action Group
- Improved local services
- Established a system of rigorous monitoring

Service agencies felt that a sense of ownership and pride had developed in the project, but this is a fairly low-level, low-cost initiative, with no devolved budgets, no resident management of services and, as yet, only a limited impact on capacity building a wider cross-section of residents than those directly involved.

Source: Cole et al (2000)

❏ Services covered by some current estate agreements

Services	Monsall, Manchester (Guinness Trust)	Cheetwood (Guinness Trust)	Old Fold, Gateshead (Gateshead MBC)	Huddleston Close, London (Bethnal Green and Victoria Park HA)	Fordyce Estate (Home Group)	Broadwater Farm (LB of Haringey)	Blackbird Leys, Oxford (Ealing Family HA)	Norton Grange, Teeside (Tees Valley Housing Group)	Zsara (SPACE)	Runcorn (Liverpool Housing Trust/CDS)	Gipsyville (Sanctuary HA)	Manor, Sheffield (North British HA)
Repairs	●	●	●	●	●	●	●	●		●		●
Nuisance/good neighbour	●	●	●	●	●	●	●	●	●	●	●	
Street cleaning	●		●			●	●	●		●		●
Grassed areas	●		●			●	●	●				●
Lettings	●	●								●	●	
Rubbish	●					●			●			●
Crime			●					●	●	●		
Empty homes	●	●	●							●		
Security				●		●						
Lighting								●				●
Rent collection		●						●				
Animals/pets								●	●		●	
Jobs/training								●				
Feedback/comments	●	●	●	●		●						●

Source: Cole, I et al (2000)

❑ Carrots and sticks

One of the principal aims of Neighbourhood Management is to secure for local communities reliable, high quality and cost effective services which meet both their needs and expectations. What can be done if service provision fails to live up to residents' expectations, or falls below the standards set out in the Neighbourhood Action Plan is a tricky issue.

Sanctions are unlikely to be a popular option with most service providers. Neighbourhood managers are likely to prefer negotiated solutions to service deficiencies, rather than resorting to sanctions against organisations that may well be partners in the Neighbourhood Management process.

Carrots and sticks at Broadwater Farm London Borough of Haringey

All service providers on the estate now have agreements or contracts with the local authority which are monitored closely. Rectification notices are sent out if services fall below the agreed standard. Providers are given ten days to rectify problems after a first notice. A second notice is then sent out; no action leads to an immediate report to an assistant director of housing. Payment for the service is then withheld.

Only one service provider has got this far through the process, which perhaps suggests that the sanctions arrangements are reasonably effective.

The estate caretakers pick up contractor delays quickly. The Neighbourhood Office then chases people immediately. Much depends on personal contact by people who are constantly on-the-spot. Other management approaches may be less effective.

Establishing clear and transparent criteria for monitoring and reporting service performance will undoubtedly help. Many problems can probably be sorted out by negotiation, but residents may well have a different perspective. Empowered communities may find it hard to accept that professionals resolving problems quietly behind the scenes is the best way forward; they may prefer to put in place some robust and transparent sanctions to ensure that services are up to scratch.

CHAPTER 8

MONITORING AND EVALUATION

What this Chapter is about

This chapter sets out initial ideas on how organisations involved in Neighbourhood Management should monitor and evaluate its impact, including:

- How current DTLR guidance for NDC pathfinders can be adapted
- Getting the basic principles right
- Involving local communities in the evaluation process
- A potential evaluation framework for lead agencies
- New ways of disseminating the results

Monitoring and evaluating Neighbourhood Management requires a change in the current approaches and methodologies used for neighbourhood regeneration. Whilst the approach to neighbourhood regeneration has changed significantly in recent years, the evaluation techniques have not kept pace. The guidance on evaluating New Deal for Communities programmes from DTLR does, however, make some significant steps forward. It can usefully inform an evaluative approach to Neighbourhood Management.

The particular aims of Neighbourhood Management, and the processes required to make it work, need an approach and methodology which will not only measure success against targets but, perhaps more importantly, also provide robust evidence of what works, for whom and in what circumstances. The purpose of evaluation in this context needs to be as much about learning and development as accountability.

This section of the Guide therefore looks at the issues for housing professionals which are likely to be involved in evaluating Neighbourhood Management. It considers some of the basic principles which should influence the development of evaluative methodologies, and some of the key elements which might comprise them. Finally, it looks at the need for better dissemination of evaluation findings to promote learning and inform practice.

❑ Evaluating Neighbourhood Management

The guidance issued by DTLR to the potential Neighbourhood Management pathfinders suggests that those that are successful will be asked to set out both their long term aims and short term outputs and performance standards in their detailed strategies, against which they will be monitored on implementation. Significantly, the Government does not intend to be prescriptive about these measures, although it will expect them to be agreed with the local Government Office for the Region.

This approach reflects that taken with the NDC programmes and it seems likely that the further detailed guidance will be on similar lines. If so, there will be much that is conventional in regeneration evaluation – the analysis of outcomes and impacts; addressing sustainability and additionality; the assessment of value for money; and the analysis of implementation processes. However, there are also a number of aspects of NDC evaluation guidance that are more innovative:

- National evaluation which will work alongside and support the local partnership in order to avoid a top-down approach
- The opportunity to take a long-term approach – a methodology which is sufficiently robust to be applied over a minimum period of 10 years and sufficiently flexible to be adapted to changing circumstances
- An emphasis on outcomes (views and attitudes) rather than outputs (facts and figures)
- Applying an action research approach, where immediate remedial action results from findings during the evaluative process
- An emphasis on analysing links with and the potential added value of, other area-based initiatives and mainstream programmes and services
- Identifying what works and how
- Early feedback on quick wins and initial lessons to inform spend and priority areas for action
- Health checks, where external advice and support is provided

The focus of evaluation is clearly moving away from simply assessing goal achievement – the extent to which a policy or programme meets its intended objectives – towards understanding how and why a policy or programme works and the circumstances in which it works best or least. Most practitioners will welcome the change.

It is still too early for any substantive feedback on the implementation of NDC evaluations, so the Neighbourhood Management pathfinders will, to some extent, be flying blind. A useful starting point is the evaluative framework for NDCs, although these were initially based on top-down outcome indicators; a more bottom up approach may emerge in the future.

Also of use are the suggested key questions for evaluating Neighbourhood Management, set out in the PAT4 report:

- Process: was the programme implemented as planned?
- Impact: did it make a difference to priority problems? (i.e. are there lower levels of crime, joblessness, ill-health and underachievement? have services improved? have other community priorities been addressed?
- Cost benefits: were the benefits greater than the costs?
- Credibility: was the programme credible with the community?
- Durability: did the benefits last?
- Replicability: can it be developed in other areas?

What will be required is new and creative thinking in two areas. The first is how to develop the process of evaluation – how it is carried out – to reflect the key features of Neighbourhood Management, such as community involvement and leadership and local delivery of a range of services. The second is how best to ensure that the component parts of the evaluation – what it measures, such as the collection of information, and the setting of indicators and targets – reflect the specific objectives of Neighbourhood Management.

❑ Getting the basic principles right

So there is a significant challenge in evaluating Neighbourhood Management. The early programmes will be required to design, establish and apply evaluative approaches and methodologies which cover new territory. The differences inherent in Neighbourhood Management as against any previous area renewal programmes will require new ways of measuring impact and change. On the plus side, this presents the opportunity to develop approaches and methodologies which are tailored to local circumstance and capacity. It will be essential, however, that the overall approach and framework reflects the key elements.

There are some basic principles which should guide the development of evaluation methodologies for Neighbourhood Management by:

- Developing a system which judges results rather than the means of achieving the results, which should be diverse and locally defined
- Recognising that the main interests to be evaluated are those of the local community, not those of service providers

- Actively involving residents in the process, including those from black and minority ethnic communities and other under-represented groups
- Developing a system which measures improvement in the delivery of individual services as well as how effective they are in working together
- Developing an evaluation framework which encourages 'equifinality', meaning that there are multiple routes to a single end
- Ensuring any evaluation framework is based on 'specificity', that is, it can be tailored according to local circumstance and need
- Developing local targets and indicators which can be linked to national priorities, policies and indicators
- Developing local targets and indicators which are cross-cutting
- Amplifying the action research based approach, to emphasise the value of action on the ground to improve programmes as a result of feedback both through the evaluative process and generally
- Establishing a comprehensive dissemination strategy, to ensure widespread learning

In general, evaluation needs to become a mainstream part of Neighbourhood Management programmes, intrinsically useful in determining planning and informing change, rather than a time-consuming bureaucratic process imposed by funders for purposes of financial control. It needs to become a positive rather than a negative tool.

❏ Involving local communities

One of the key issues here will be the greater involvement of local people in the evaluative process, both in its administration and as providers of source information and data. This is often called participatory evaluation. It means that the approach and methodologies are driven either wholly or in part by the desire to involve local people at all stages of the evaluative process. The key elements are:

- It involves participants in learning evaluation logic and skills, it builds capacity
- The participants 'own' the evaluation
- Participants focus on the process and outcomes they consider important and to which they are committed
- Participants work together as a group, supported as necessary
- All aspects of the evaluation are understandable and meaningful to participants
- Internal self-accountability is highly valued, the evaluation supports participants' accountability to themselves and their community first, and external accountability secondarily

- Professional staff are facilitators and a learning resource
- The perspectives of participants are recognised and valued
- Status differences between the professional staff and participants are reduced

Source: Adapted from Patton, MQ (1997)

Ways in which this might be achieved include:

- Involvement in defining the approach and methodologies to be used in the evaluative process
- Support to carry out parts of the evaluation themselves, through assembling baseline information, surveys, interviews, appraisals
- Shadowing of professional evaluation staff

and, as key elements of the evaluation, including qualitative information, such as:

- Case studies, real-life examples of an individual and/or group experience
- Attitude and behaviour statements, completed by individuals and/or groups at key points based on peoples' day to day experience and measuring changes over time in their lives
- Video portraits, short films presenting the views of individuals
- 'Life scripts', expressing feelings and experiences
- Photographs, taken by individuals and/or groups to show what they like and don't like about their community

Many of these techniques are particularly useful in drawing in the experiences and views of children, young people, people from black and minority ethnic communities, people with disabilities and older people. They can also be used to generate discussions, exhibitions and debates outside the evaluative process which can have a beneficial impact on community capacity and cohesion.

❑ Towards an evaluative methodology for Neighbourhood Management

Effective evaluation requires baseline information on the local conditions/situations which the programme is aiming to improve, clear objectives setting out the changes the programme is aiming to make, clear definition of intended beneficiaries and appropriate indicators to measure change. Taking into account the principles outlined above, an evaluative methodology for Neighbourhood Management might be created using the following building blocks.

Baseline information

Collecting baseline information, which provides a picture of the situation before the programme was implemented, is a first step in the process. Any previous difficulties associated with collecting information at a local level need to be addressed at this stage. Data collected and held at a national level on key indicators is now becoming available at area level (see Chapter 7). Regeneration programmes prior to Neighbourhood Management have resulted in a huge amount of information at a regional level, although this is often dispersed. The neighbourhood renewal teams in the Regional Government Offices have a clear role here in assembling data and information which can both be added to the central pool administered by the new Skills and Knowledge team and provided to Neighbourhood Management programmes regionally to advise on policy and practice.

Locally, resident surveys, questionnaires, and planning events have provided detailed information about an area, often in a qualitative form. It may also be necessary to commission new pieces of work to collate specific information. There are clear opportunities here for involving residents in the collection of data and information and even, as the East Brighton NDC programme intends, to create local employment, particularly in the on-going updating and review of information through monitoring over the life of the programme.

Strategic goal

Using the definition of Neighbourhood Management provided in Chapter 1, the strategic goal of a Neighbourhood Management programme could be to:

> *narrow the gap between the neighbourhood and the rest of the locality by dramatically improving outcomes, especially in employment, education, health, crime and housing.*

Overall aims

Aims will then need to be set to achieve this goal. These should be tailored to local conditions and circumstance. Taking the key principles of Neighbourhood Management, community involvement and leadership and service improvement, there are five main areas within which local aims could be developed:

- **Influence** – steps to increase the power of local people to negotiate in the political process of resource allocation and application through the development of strong democratic structures
- **Inclusion** – steps towards equity for all sections of the community, including those commonly excluded by virtue of their race, ethnicity, age, disability, gender, or other social and economic factors

- **Communication** – steps towards implementing clear information channels, including transparent and accessible policies and procedures
- **Capacity** – steps towards strengthening the skills, knowledge, understanding and access to resources of individuals, groups and organisations within communities, including leadership development
- **Quality of life** – steps towards improving the quality of life for an area's residents, particularly in [relation] to employment, education, health, crime and housing

Source: adapted from Knight, B (2001)

■ Specific objectives

These overall aims then translate into objectives, or targets to assess the scale of impact the changes measured have achieved. So within each category a range of specific targets would be set against which impact and change could be measured. Included here would be the specific target groups that the programme is aiming to benefit, which may include young people, black and minority ethnic communities, people with disabilities, and unemployed people. The targets should indicate dates for achievement, or milestones, against which progress can be monitored.

■ Indicators

The instruments which enable targets to be assessed and measured are the indicators. A useful starting point will be those used for City Challenge and SRB (published by DTLR) as well as, if possible, those adopted by the NDC round 1 partnerships. Indicators need to cover outputs (facts and figures, often called quantitative data) and outcomes (perceptions, views, attitudes, often called qualitative information). The emphasis is increasingly towards outcomes.

However, the particular overall goal of Neighbourhood Management will require new indicators, derived from both local conditions and national guidance. The key will be to develop indicators that are cross-cutting.

Of particular use here will be:
- The Audit Commission's *Voluntary Quality of Life and Cross-cutting Indicators for Local Authorities*
- Those identified in the National Strategy for Neighbourhood Renewal
- Those being used by the local authorities involved in local Public Sector Agreement pilots
- Best Value and Audit Commission Performance Indicators for 2001/02
- The DTLR's *Local Quality of Life Counts – A handbook for a menu of local indicators of sustainable development*

- The Government's main quality of life indicators
- Those available locally and regionally from specific sectors, including housing, health, education, crime and safety, and employment

❏ Dissemination and learning lessons

There are a number of audiences to consider, each of which will require the information in different formats if it is to be widely accessible:

- Board members
- Staff
- The local community
- Partner organisations and agencies
- Other Neighbourhood Management programmes and regeneration projects generally
- Policy makers and planners regionally and centrally

In some instances, traditional methods of dissemination will be appropriate – reports, briefing sessions, articles in newsletters, or publications. In others, a more face to face approach will be required – away days, presentations, open days or planning events. The additional dimension now available to encourage much greater access and easier, quicker dissemination is that provided by e-government initiatives and, in particular, the national website proposed as part of the Skills and Knowledge team due to be operational by March 2002.

The new Skills and Knowledge team at the Neighbourhood Renewal Unit has an important role generally in dissemination. The proposed knowledge management system will provide a central point for the collection and dissemination of information about what works, and what doesn't, in Neighbourhood Management. It will link into sources of evidence from other departments, outside bodies, and regional, local and neighbourhood feedback. The Skills and Knowledge team will have a close link with the Regional Government Offices, which can act as a clearing house at regional level for information and feedback. The team will also ensure that advice is available to partnerships and communities that want it, including the possibility of 'residents' consultancy'.

It is proposed that regional panels of advisers are established to provide advice, support and guidance to regeneration partnerships generally. These are likely to be piloted in the North-East, East Midlands and South-West regions. They will provide a complement to the learning networks of regeneration partnerships being developed by some Government Offices. In addition, the National

Network of Regeneration Partnerships has a national role in bringing together partnerships to share expertise and practice.

Evaluation is therefore not an end in itself – it is only useful if it achieves better results. For this to happen, the findings of evaluations have to be disseminated, locally, regionally and nationally.

Regeneration Exchange

Regeneration Exchange covers the North-East of England and provides support, advice and guidance to regeneration partnerships in the region. It is supported by the Regional Government Office and One NorthEast, the Regional Development Agency, through a mixture of SRB and NDC funding. The Exchange is based at Sunderland City Council, which is the accountable body for the funding. It also has an office on Teeside. It reports to an independent steering committee of representatives from regeneration partnerships from the public, private, voluntary and community sectors.

It is a free service and responds to requests from around 600 current practitioners for information and advice on all aspects of regeneration and is growing by around 50 members a month. It has four working groups comprised of practitioners dealing with specific aspects of regeneration, including monitoring and evaluation, Best Value, community capacity and the environment. Information on practice is collected both from within the region and nationally. The Exchange is a member of the National Network of Regeneration Partnerships and has contributed to feasibility work by DTLR to establish a regional panel of advisers.

Chapter 9

Neighbourhood Management poses important new challenges for housing professionals and others working in the housing environment. They need to get to grips with them now and not wait to see how things pan out. The new approach to neighbourhood renewal opens up the prospect of today's housing managers becoming tomorrow's neighbourhood managers. But this will not happen unless those delivering housing services are ready for fundamental change. Without such change, Neighbourhood Management may become a missed opportunity for the housing profession.

Neighbourhood Management is still experimental. No-one can be sure how successful it will be or how it might develop as time goes by. But it is without question at the core of the Government's strategic approach to tackling social exclusion in our deprived neighbourhoods. It is unlikely to be a policy initiative which will be shelved after the pilot stage. Neighbourhood Management is here to stay. Housing professionals who do not engage early in the process are likely to be left behind.

Neighbourhood Management is clearly not an activity which can be successfully carried out in isolation. By its nature it requires new and challenging ways of working, new linkages and partnerships and a variety of joined up activities. What happens in neighbourhoods must 'fit' with what happens in the wider context – through Local Strategic Partnerships, public service agreements and regional strategies (see Chapter 3).

But is Neighbourhood Management enough? Is it sufficient to focus the effort on the delivery of services and making these more effective and relevant to communities, through local co-ordination and budgeting? It is an important question.

Neighbourhood Management will be a much more powerful tool in the long run if it not only deals with the delivery of services, but also facilitates the development of local plans and strategies. A truly comprehensive and radical approach to neighbourhood sustainability needs to bring together local control of services and investment in renewal programmes. Putting local communities in the driving seat in this respect raises the possibility of community-generated neighbourhood development plans and frameworks and a specific focus on community-owned assets. There are already some useful models around.

This joined up and bottom up approach to Neighbourhood Management and renewal may be some way off, but it is not too far over the horizon. One thing is certain – the neighbourhood agenda is unlikely to begin and end with the management of services.

A P P E N D I X 1

H OUSING G REEN P APER –
M AIN P ROPOSALS

- Promoting a stronger strategic role for local authorities (as distinct from their traditional landlord role), linking housing and the environment with policies on the other four key areas of health, education, crime, and unemployment

- Supporting sustainable home ownership, including enabling social landlords to support the improvement of private sector housing and linking improvements to Housing Benefit to helping unemployed homeowners move into work

- Raising the standards of private landlords, through the licensing of privately rented homes by local authorities and placing conditions on the receipt of Housing Benefit by bad private landlords

- Improving the quality of social housing and housing management, through stock transfer, Best Value and arms-length companies

- Improvements to the delivery of affordable housing, relating to clearly identified current and future local demand, improvements to the quality of construction of social housing, and mixed tenure developments

- Promoting new lettings policies, which support movement across local authority boundaries, and between RSLs and local authorities, targeting support on the most vulnerable households, and encouraging flexible lettings policies to reflect local needs and problems

- Strengthening the protection available to homeless families, through extending the statutory safety-net to wider groups of homeless people, giving greater flexibility to social landlords to link availability in their stock to providing housing to non-priority homeless people and more sustainable solutions for all homeless people, and requiring a multi-agency approach to homelessness

- Reviewing tenure arrangements to ensure security for long-term social tenants, by unifying the secure and assured tenancy regimes, and providing new flexibilities which enable social landlords to make better use of their stock

- Maintaining rents at affordable levels, holding most rents at current levels and closing the gap between rents charged by local authorities and RSLs

- Restructuring rents, in order to better reflect the size, quality and location of homes, as well as regional earnings and running costs, phased over 10 years

- Improving the Housing Benefit system, by reducing bureaucracy and complexity, tackling fraud and error, and increasing the incentive to work by targeting earning disregards

APPENDIX 2

POTENTIAL SOURCES OF FUNDING FOR COMMUNITY INVOLVEMENT IN NEIGHBOURHOOD MANAGEMENT

Government Departments

Government Departments provide a range of funds for communities and also fund intermediaries involved in community-based projects and programmes. The main current programmes are set out below.

1. The DTLR *Tenant Empowerment Grant* programme:
    *   Focused on local authority tenants
    *   To capacity build tenants' organisations, enabling them to play a key role in Best Value, particularly in those areas where participation has been slow to get off the ground
    *   Funds distributed through a national network of specialist intermediaries, who provide local support

2. The Home Office's *Community Resource Fund*:
    *   Administered by the Community Development Foundation and the Association of Community Trusts and Foundations (ACTAF, now known as the Community Foundation Network or CFN)
    *   A small fund currently being piloted by the Active Community Unit of the Home Office
    *   30 pilot projects nationwide
    *   Allocation of £5,000 each, providing grants of up to £500 to small and new community groups to help them get established

3. The Department for Education and Skills *Community Champions Fund*:
    *   Launched in late 1999
    *   Aimed at supporting individuals who can make a difference in their communities through formal and informal training, access to information and learning opportunities
    *   Being delivered throughout England, with administration carried out by Government Offices for the Regions

4. The Department for Education and Skills *Neighbourhood Support Fund*:
   - Also launched in late 1999
   - Aimed at bringing disadvantaged young people into learning and work
   - Targeted at 500 community-based projects in the 40 most deprived local authorities in England
   - £13.8 million over three years is specifically available for allocation directly to community organisations, and this part of the fund is administered through the Community Development Foundation

5. Department for Education and Skills *Millennium Volunteers*:
   - Launched in January 1999 and now in its third round
   - Aim of the programme is to encourage 16-24 year olds to commit 200 hours of planned and recognised voluntary activity which benefits themselves and the wider community
   - Programme has a budget of £48 million in England

Government sponsored Public Sector Agencies

6. The Regional Development Agencies (RDAs) have a strong focus on economic investment. Currently responsible for the delivery of
   - The *Community Investment Fund* – a useful source of capital finance for a range of community projects, previously operated by English Partnerships. This is no longer a ring-fenced budget

7. The Housing Corporation:
   - Responsible for the funding and regulation of housing associations in England, many of whom have a substantial stake in local communities, through ownership and management of social housing
   - Running a pilot programme of *Community Training and Enabling Grants*, aimed at assisting residents to play an effective role, with registered social landlords, in developing proposals for the future of their housing and neighbourhoods

8. Regional Offices of the NHS Executive have a small, but growing role in funding communities. *Health Action Zones*, set up to work with community groups and other stakeholders to deliver health improvements in target areas, have resources for capacity building and community development work, as do the new Primary Care Groups

9. Regional Arts Boards have a small role in capacity building, through their support for a range of community arts programmes

10. *Education Action Zones* and *Sure Start* programmes, administered by the Department for Education and Skills, have a potentially important role in community development and capacity building, although they were not set up to provide direct funds to communities

Local Authorities

11. Local authorities:
    - Have traditionally had a key role in funding communities, primarily through provision of grants to community organisations, running of community centres and employment of community development workers
    - Whilst non-financial forms of support are still much in evidence, and local authorities play a leading role in most SRB and New Deal for Communities programmes, funding restrictions have substantially reduced their ability to sustain grant programmes. Strategic partnerships with other funders have helped to plug some of the more obvious gaps

European Funding Programmes

12. The European Union:
    - Current round of the *European Regional Development Fund* (ending 1999) was used to support a wide range of projects in priority areas, some involving the development of local community partnerships, community training and a range of self help projects
    - Community involvement is a more explicit theme of the 2000 – 2006 Structural Fund programme
    - *URBAN Initiative* (European Regional Development Fund) was specifically targeted on community capacity building in inner city communities (also concluded 1999). Key themes included improving information and communication within local communities and supporting the development and capacity of community organisations
    - *European Social Fund*'s (ESF) Objective 3, Priority 4 Programme is currently being used to build the capacity of small, locally based organisations involved in community training and job creation initiatives – a relatively new aspect of ESF programmes, which have, in the past, mainly concerned themselves with mainstream training for unemployed individuals. 4% of the UK ESF budget was set aside for capacity building local community organisations within this programme
    - All European funding programmes carry with them problems of long lead in times and particular difficulties with matching funding, which continue to pose serious problems for local communities trying to access them. But some solutions to these problems are now being tested

National Lottery Programmes

13. The Community Fund, formerly the National Lottery Charities Board, is the largest grant making body in Britain:

    - Runs two main programmes, administered on a regional basis – *Community Involvement* and *Poverty and Disadvantage*
    - Many of its grants support a broad range of community initiatives
    - Some grants are made England-wide
    - Board also operates a small grants programme – *Awards for All* – providing amounts of between £500 and £5,000 for smaller scale community activities, with no deadlines or priority themes
    - The Board embarked on a regional capacity-building programme for the voluntary and community sectors in late 1999

14. The New Opportunities Fund distributes a share of the money raised by the National Lottery to health, education and environment projects across the UK:

    - By working in partnership, aims to support sustainable projects that will encourage community participation and complement national strategies and programmes
    - Has specific targets for each of its programmes
    - Can fund capacity building as part of projects which meet its criteria

15. The Arts Council of England runs its own Lottery programme as well as providing grant aid to arts based organisations. Since late 1998, the focus of its Lottery capital programme has shifted to projects in deprived areas and this is likely to be a stronger feature of its future programme. Half the awards within the 'Arts for Everyone' small grants programme now go to locally based voluntary or community groups

Community and voluntary sector intermediary agencies

16. Intermediary organisations provide facilities and resources targeted at increasing the capacity of community groups, including:

    - Advice, support and expertise e.g. on management, organisational, funding, legal and technical issues
    - Resources, such as office equipment
    - Training and information courses
    - Opportunities for community groups to network, thus sharing skills, information and enabling joint working
    - A developmental role, assisting with the establishment of new groups, giving on-going support and supporting voluntary activity in communities

- Can raise issues of race and gender and help ensure that groups operate on the basis of equality
- Some offer technical services, such as community planning and architecture

17. Intermediaries rarely provide direct funding for local communities, although some act as administrators or gatekeepers for major funding bodies. Many are funded by the Home Office Active Community Unit, which has awarded £11.4 million for 2000/2001 to increase voluntary and community involvement and support the development of active communities. A further £12 million is administered by the Home Office's Race Equality Unit, through the *Connecting Communities* programme, to empower marginalised minority ethnic communities. A further £1.5 million over three years is being used to build a regional network for the black and minority ethnic sector

Key intermediaries involved in supporting community initiatives include:

18. The Development Trusts Association (DTA):
    - Member organisation
    - Organised on a regional basis in England
    - Has been managing two small funds with a capacity building focus; an *Asset Base Development Fund* (financed through DTLR's Special Grants programme, requires a 50% contribution from applicants) and a *Knowledge and Skills Exchange* (funded by the Baring Foundation). Both aim to equip communities with the understanding they need to establish Development Trusts

19. Community Matters (National Federation of Community Organisations):
    - Nearly 1000 members
    - Runs a Community Consultancy Service, using experienced practitioners within its network to work with community groups to help build their capacity
    - Does not provide direct funding to communities

20. The 250 local Councils for Voluntary Service:
    - Provide a resource for local communities and often play an important role in capacity building, primarily through the provision of information, advice and training
    - Supported by the National Association of Councils for Voluntary Service, funded mainly by the Home Office and the DTLR

21. The British Association of Settlements and Social Action Centres (*BASSAC*):
    - National organisation with a network of 78 members
    - Focus on locally-based multi-purpose centres involved in helping deprived communities bring about social change

22. The Black Training and Enterprise Group (*BTEG*):
    - National black organisation established in 1991 by representatives from the black voluntary sector
    - Contributes to the economic regeneration of black communities in the UK
    - Represents over 200 organisations
    - Focuses on training, employment, enterprise and regeneration

23. The Scarman Trust:
    - Currently administering the *Community Champions Fund* on behalf of three Government Offices for the Regions
    - Provides support to a wide range of individuals in communities, through the Millennium Volunteers – a Department for Education and Skills initiative – and the 'Can Do' programmes

24. A number of other national organisations provide information and advice to enable local urban communities to access resources. They include:
    - Urban Forum
    - Church Urban Fund
    - The Standing Conference on Community Development
    - The National Association of Volunteer Bureaux
    - The newly established Regional Voluntary Sector Networks are also beginning to play an important role in capacity building work

Private Trusts and Foundations

26. Many Trusts and Foundations support community-based initiatives, ranging from well-known national bodies, such as the Baring, Calouste Gulbenkian and Joseph Rowntree Foundations, to small local charities with limited grant giving roles. Most wish to see tangible outputs for their investment – something to which community capacity building work is not well suited. Consequently, not enough of this money may be getting down to where it really counts. Nevertheless, considerable investment is going into helping intermediaries build their capacity, both internally and through developing networks. The umbrella body for these trusts and foundations is the Community Foundation Network (CFN), formerly the Association of Community Trusts and Foundations.

Community Foundations

27. CFN supports a growing network of 29 community foundations which between them make local grants of around £22 million per annum and hold endowment funds of more than £91 million, raised primarily from charitable trusts, companies, public bodies and individuals. Nearly half of these Community Foundations have assets of more than £1 million; seven of them have assets of over £5 million

Registered Social Landlords

28. RSLs working in neighbourhoods and particularly those with a neighbourhood focus may have revenue funds available to support community engagement in Neighbourhood Management initiatives. Latest estimates suggest that four out of every five registered social landlords are engaged in community investment of some kind:

    - They are investing in communities themselves, through the provision of staff resources for community development, financing of tenants' and residents' groups, active support for tenant or community-led projects
    - They are securing external funding from a variety of sources to support a broad range of community sustainability initiatives
    - Some are diversifying their business to prioritise community investment

Source: Duncan, P and Thomas, S (2001b)

Appendix 3

List of 20 pathfinders July 2001

Region	Project	Local Authority	H/H / Pop	Type
London	Woolwich Common Neighbourhood Initiative	Greenwich	4700/10300	Metropolitan
	Go Gospel Oak	Camden	4831/7279	Metropolitan
South East	Great Hollington	Hastings	4000/10400	Urban, seaside resort
South West	Community Counts	Gloucester City	4941/12154	Market/ county town
	Building Boscombe Together	Bournemouth	/ 2500	Urban, seaside resort
West Mids	Knutton Cross Neighbourhood Management Initiative	Newcastle under Lyme	2660/6000	Urban district
	Reviving the Heart of Burton	East Staffordshire	3870/9700	Urban district
East Mids	Kirkby speaks – a neighbourhood shows the way	Ashfield	4287/10999	Urban district, ex-coalfield
	A better deal for Staveley	Chesterfield	4379/ 0061	Mixed urban/ rural, coalfield
East	Interlock- Northlands Park	Basildon	3510/ 193	Urban district, new town

Region	Project	Local Authority	H/H / Pop	Type
Yorkshire & Humber	Getting the best for Dewsbury	West Kirklees	4942/14329	Metropolitan
	Kendray Initiative	Barnsley	/6000	Metropolitan
	Eastwell and Springwell Gardens Neighbourhood	Rotherham	2600/ 6000	Metropolitan
North West	Great Lever Neighbourhood Renewal	Bolton	3300/8000	Metropolitan
	Taking Care of Hattersley	Tameside	2500/7000	Metropolitan
	Blacon Together	Chester	5900/ 14540	Market/ county town
	Pulling Together for Poulton	Lancaster City Council	2050/5500	Rural, seaside resort
North East	The Making of Parkfield	Stockton on Tees	3100/7000	Metropolitan/ town centre
	Stanley Green Corridor – Improving Services in partnership	Derwentside	4732/11219	Semi-rural, ex-coalfield
	Coastal Area Neighbourhood Approach	Easington	4024/	Coalfield, coastal

Source: DTLR press release, (2001)

APPENDIX 4

GLOSSARY OF TERMS

Additionality – additional benefits which are brought to a project via funding or other methods

Action Teams for Jobs – currently based in 40 areas across Great Britain including 15 Employment Zones. The Budget 2001 statement announced an extension of existing Action Teams until the end of March 2004. Action Teams for Jobs offer opportunities for jobless people living in areas where employment rates are low, unemployment is high and where people find it difficult to work because of personal histories, where they live etc.

Capacity Building – strengthening the skills and abilities of partners, professionals and the community

Citizens' Juries – representative group of non-experts who deliberate an issue, cross-examine witnesses and produce a report

Community development – providing local communities and individuals with the support they need to engage with professionals and their agencies on an equal basis

Communities of interest – a community of people who do not live in the same locality but who share a common interest

Community Lettings Plans – initiatives developed in response to local circumstances. They differ from mainstream lettings policies as they may give priority to people who want to live in the area, allocate properties to applicants in non-priority groups or restrict eligibility for housing etc. Any community lettings initiatives developed by housing associations/registered social landlords need to comply with requirements set by the regulator. In addition, any equality implications should be carefully considered. For instance, giving extra priority to local people may exclude black and minority ethnic people from areas where they are already under-represented

Connexions – a service launched across England to provide guidance, advice and support to young people about life, education and career choices. It is intended that eventually advice will be available from personal advisers, via the website and a telephone service

Consumer Champions – network of departmental Ministers engaged in improving the responsiveness of services in deprived areas

Education Action Zones – a cluster of schools – usually a mix of 20 primary, secondary and special schools – working in partnership with the Local Education Authority, local parents, businesses etc. Partnership will encourage 'innovative approaches to tackling disadvantage and raising standards. They may also link in with Education Action Zones, Health or Employment zones and with projects funded by the Single Regeneration Budget

Employment Zones – part of the Government's Welfare to Work strategy. They enable local partnerships 'to develop ways of helping the long term unemployed back into work.' They concentrate on geographical areas with high levels of long-term unemployed. Employment Zones also try to combine as many of the funding sources as legislation permits

Excellence in Cities (EiC) – a targeted programme to bring additional resources to address the needs of core urban areas. Specifically directed at transforming secondary education in major cities. Its main strands are also being piloted at primary level. Working in partnership with the EiC, Local Education Authorities and their schools are putting in place enhanced educational opportunities for gifted and talented children, access to learning mentors to help children overcome barriers to learning etc.

Health Action Zones (HAZ) – partnerships between the NHS, local authorities (including social services), community groups and the voluntary and business sectors. Their aim is to develop and implement a health strategy to deliver measurable improvements in public health and in the outcomes and quality of treatment and care

Health Improvement Plans/Programmes (HImP) – Each Health Authority is required to draw up HImPs which detail action to improve health and healthcare locally. Although led by the Health Authority, they must work in partnership with NHS Trusts, Primary Care Groups, the local authority and 'engage' other local interests

Neighbourhood Renewal Fund – targets have been set by the Government to improve outcomes in relation to crime, health, employment, education, and housing and environment. The purpose of the additional funding is to help local authorities and their partners to begin to improve core public services. The additional resources (available for over three years to the 88 most deprived areas in England) may also be used for Neighbourhood Management

New Deal for Schools – a five-year programme announced in July 1997 to improve the condition of school buildings and enhance facilities for technology, thereby helping to raise educational standards

New Deal Innovation Fund – New Deal is a key element of the Government's Welfare to Work Agenda. The programme made progress over its first year but there was a desire to achieve more. This prompted the development of the New Deal Continuous Improvement Strategy. Part of that strategy is to encourage the development of innovative ways of locally designing and delivering New Deal. The New Deal Innovation Fund was established in order to develop projects which support priorities to achieve equality of outcomes for people from ethnic minority backgrounds, increase geographical mobility, improve retention in jobs, to increase job outcomes in neighbourhoods with higher than average unemployment rates etc.

Pathfinders – pilot schemes which find and assess models for new ways of working

Planning for Real – a consultation and involvement technique.It uses a simple model as a focus for people to put forward and prioritise ideas as to how their areas can be improved. Kits and instructions can be supplied by the Neighbourhood Initiatives Foundation

Personal Medical Services Pilots (PMS Pilot) – the General Medical Services provided by a General Practitioner (GP) are normally provided under a standard national contract between GPs and the Secretary of Health. A PMS Pilot allows GPs and other NHS staff or organisations to contract for such services under an alternative arrangement with their local health authority or Primary Care Trust

Primary Care Trusts – Primary Care Groups consist of family doctors and community nurses who contribute to the local Health Improvement Programme and they have a budget which reflect their population's share of the available resources for hospital and community health services etc. It is however possible for Primary Care Groups to become independent. Such Trusts could be managed by a board of GPs, community nurses and managers etc.

Single Regeneration Budget (SRB) – in 1994, a number of programmes from several Government Departments were brought together in order to streamline assistance which was available for regeneration. SRB supports regeneration initiatives in England which are carried out by local regeneration partnerships. SRB partnerships are expected to involve a diverse range of local organisations in the management of the scheme. SRBs are administered at a regional level by the Regional Development Agencies and, in London, by the London Development Agency. Partnerships bid for various rounds of assistance and each SRB programme lasts for seven years. The types of bids differ from place to place, but can include a bid to reduce crime and drug abuse and improve community safety

Spaces for Sport and Art – part of the Government's strategy for sport, the scheme aims to improve the number and quality of facilities in areas of social deprivation to give better access to sport and the arts and to help efforts aimed at social inclusion. 65 local authorities were initially invited to bid to improve their arts and sports facilities

Sport Action Zones – under the Sport England (English Sports Council) plan, certain areas of high economic and social deprivation will be designated Sports Action Zones and targeted for improvement. The intention is to ensure that people within those areas are given the chance to be involved in sport. Providing local communities with access to school facilities at affordable prices and building strong links between schools, sports clubs and voluntary groups is considered to be important

Sure Start – a Government programme to tackle child poverty and social exclusion. Local programmes work with parents and parents-to-be to improve children's life chances through better access to: family support, advice on nurturing, health services and early learning

The Children's Fund – a part of the Government's strategy to tackle child poverty and social exclusion. The Fund will support services to identify children and young people who are showing early signs of disturbance and provide them and their families with support to 'get back on track'. Its aim is to prevent children falling into drug abuse, truancy, exclusion, unemployment and crime

The Learning and Skills Council – responsible for funding and planning education and training for over 16 year olds in England

Adapted in part from the following:

www.cabinet-office.gov.uk/seu
Cabinet Office, Social Exclusion Unit – Neighbourhood Renewal Fund

www.culture.gov.uk/sport/search2.asp?Name=/sport/press/2000/dcms006.txt
Department for Culture, Media and Sport, Sports Action Zones

www.culture.gov.uk/cgi-bin/text.pl?www.culture.gov.uk/sport/intro.html
Department for Culture, Media and Sport, Spaces for Sport and Art

www.dfee.gov.uk/edaction/edaction.htm
Department for Education and Skills – Education Action Zones

www.standards.dfes.gov.uk
Department for Education and Skills- Education Action Zones and Excellence in Cities

www.dfee.gov.uk/newdeal/pt1.htm
Department for Education and Skills, New Deal for Schools

www.dfee.gov.uk/cypu/home_cf.shtml
Department for Education and Skills, Children Fund

www.doh.gov.uk/pricare/haz.htm
Department of Health – Health Action Zones

www.doh.gov.uk/pricare/pcts.htm
Department of Health – Primary Care

www.official-documents.co.uk/documents/doh/newnhs/annex.htm
Department of Health – Primary Care

www.official-documrents.co.uk/doh/newnhs/glossay.htm
Department of Health – Glossary, Health Improvement Programmes

www.doh.gov.uk/pricare/pms3rdwave.htm
Department of Health – Personal Medical Services PMS Pilot

www.surestart.gov.uk
Department for Education and Skills, Sure Start Unit

www.lifelonglearning.co.uk/etda/p3104.htm
Department for Education and Skills, New Deal Innovation Fund

www.dfee.gov.uk/actionteams
Department for Work and Pensions – Action Teams for Jobs

www.connexions.gov.uk/young.htm
Department for Education and Skills, Connexions National Unit

www.dfee.gov.uk/oldxxxempzone.htm
Department for Work and Pensions – Employment Zones

www.lsc.gov.uk/aboutus.cfm
The Learning and Skills Council

Appendix 5

Glossary of Abbreviations

BASSAC	British Association of Settlements and Social Action Centres
BTEG	Black Training and Enterprise Group
CDFI	Community Development Financial Institution
CDVCF	Community Development Venture Capital Fund
CFN	Community Foundation Network
CIH	Chartered Institute of Housing
CITC	Community Investment Tax Credit
CIV	Community Investment Vehicle
CRZ	Community Regeneration Zone
DETR	Department for the Environment, Transport and the Regions (now DTLR, see below)
DfEE	Department for Education and Employment (now DfES, see below)
DfES	Department for Education and Skills
DTA	Development Trusts Association
DTLR	Department for Transport, Local Government and the Regions
ERDF	European Regional Development Fund
ESF	European Social Fund
HARCA	Housing and Regeneration Community Association
HAT	Housing Action Trust
HPUK	Housing Potential UK
I&P Society	Industrial and Provident Society
IGP	Innovation and Good Practice Grant
IiC	Investors in Communities
JRF	Joseph Rowntree Foundation

JVC	Joint Venture Company
LGA	Local Government Association
LSP	Local Strategic Partnership
NDC	New Deal for Communities
NHF	National Housing Federation
NM	Neighbourhood Management
NRF	Neighbourhood Renewal Fund
NSNR	National Strategy for Neighbourhood Renewal
PAT	National Strategy for Neighbourhood Renewal Policy Action Team
PSA	Public Service Agreement
RDA	Regional Development Agency
RSL	Registered Social Landlord
SEU	Social Exclusion Unit
SLA	Service Level Agreement
SRB	Single Regeneration Budget

APPENDIX 6

REFERENCES AND FURTHER READING

Aldbourne Associates, (2001) *The Involvement Business: the business imperative for involving consumers in the work of registered social landlords*, The big picture series, The Housing Corporation

Atkinson, D, (2000) *Urban renaissance: a strategy for neighbourhood renewal and the welfare society*, Studley: Brewin Books

Balsall Heath Forum (2000a) *Annual report 1999-2000*, Balsall Heath Forum

Balsall Heath Forum (2001b) *The Balsall Heath neighbourhood development plan 2001-2004*, Balsall Heath Forum

Burgess, P, Hall, S, Mawson, J and Pearce, G (2001) *Devolved approaches to local governance: policy and practice in Neighbourhood Management*, Joseph Rowntree Foundation

Cabinet Office Access checklist (March 2001) www.cabinet-office.gov.uk/servicefirst/2000/joinedup/accesschecklist.htm

Cabinet Office (1999) *Modernising Government* White Paper

Chartered Institute of Housing (2000) *The Chartered Institute of Housing response to the Social Exclusion Unit's National Strategy for Neighbourhood Renewal*, Chartered Institute of Housing

Chartered Institute of Housing, Federation of Black Housing Organisations, Housing Corporation (2000) *Black and Minority Ethnic Housing Strategies – A Good Practice Guide*, Bob Blackaby and Kusminder Chahal

Cole, I, McCoulough, E and Southworth, J (2000) *Neighbourhood agreements in action: a case study of Foxwood, York*, Joseph Rowntree Foundation

Department of Environment, Transport and the Regions (DETR) (2000a) *Local Strategic Partnerships, Government guidance*, DETR

Department of Environment, Transport and the Regions (DETR) (2000b) *Our Towns and Cities: The future Delivering an Urban Renaissance*, DETR

Department of Environment, Transport and the Regions (DETR) (2000c) *Local quality of life counts – A handbook for a menu of local indicators of sustainable development*, DETR

Department of Environment, Transport and the Regions (DETR) (2000d) *Report of Policy Action Team 5 on Housing Management*, DETR

Department of Environment, Transport and the Regions (DETR) (2000e) *Report of Policy Action Team 7: Unpopular Housing*, DETR

Department of Environment Transport and the Regions (DETR) (2000f) *The housing green paper: Quality and choice, a decent home for all*, DETR

Department for Transport, Local Government and the Regions (DTLR) (2001) *News release 315*, 9 July 2001, www.press.dtlr.gov.uk/0107/0315.htm

Duncan, P (2000) *The big picture, funding for communities*, The Housing Corporation

Duncan, P and Thomas, S (2000a) *Neighbourhood regeneration, resourcing community involvement*, The Policy Press

Duncan, P and Thomas, S (2001b) Research on allocation of funding for communities, Department for Education and Skills and the Home Office

East Brighton New Deal for Communities Delivery Plan (2000) *A new deal for our community* (2000)

East Brighton New Deal for Communities Programme (2000)

Filkin, G (2000) *Starting to modernise, the change agenda for local government*, New Local Government Network

Firthmoor Community Works SRB6 Programme (2000)

Hambleton et al (1997) *Freedom within boundaries – developing effective approaches to decentralisation*, Local Government Management Board

Home Office (2000) *Report of Policy Action Team 6: Neighbourhood wardens*, The Home Office

Housing Corporation (1997) *A Housing Plus approach to achieving sustainable communities*, Housing Corporation

Housing Corporation (2001) *Modernising governance: an enabling approach*, The Housing Corporation

Housing Corporation (2001) *A Question of Diversity: black and minority ethnic staff in the RSL sector*, The Housing Corporation

Housing Corporation (2001) *A question of delivery: An evaluation of how RSLs meet the needs of black and minority ethnic communities*, The Housing Corporation

Knight, B (2001) *Raising the standard, a framework for neighbourhood renewal*, Centris

Leat, D (2000) *Holistic budgets*, Demos

Perri 6, Leat, D, Seltzer, K and Stoker G (1999) *Governing in the round: strategies for holistic government*, Demos

Local Government Association (LGA) discussion paper (2001) *The role of councillors in Neighbourhood Management*, LGA

Osborne and Gaebler (1993) *Reinventing Government*, Addison, Wesley and Renguine

Patton, M Q (1997) *Utilisation focused evaluation*, Sage

Power, A and Bergin, E (1999) *Neighbourhood Management*, Centre for Analysis of Social Exclusion, LSE

Proctor, K. (ed) (2000) *Community Led Estate Regeneration Handbook*, Churches National Housing Coalition and The Housing Corporation

Race and Housing Enquiry (2001) *Summary of written submissions*, National Housing Federation

Reid, B, Hills, S and Kane, S (2000) *Learning new tricks: education and training for organisational development in rented housing*, Sheffield Hallam University

Social Exclusion Unit (SEU) (2000a) *Report of Policy Action Team 4: Neighbourhood Management*, The Stationery Office

Social Exclusion Unit (SEU) (2001b) *A new commitment to Neighbourhood Renewal; national strategy action plan*

Social Exclusion Unit (SEU) (2001c) *National Strategy for Neighbourhood Renewal: Policy Action Team Audit*

Social Exclusion Unit (SEU) (2000d) *National Strategy for Neighbourhood Renewal; a framework for consultation*

Social Exclusion Unit (SEU) (2000e) *Report of Policy Action Team 16: learning lessons*, The Stationery Office

Stewart M (1999) *Local action to counter exclusion, report to the Local Government Research Unit*, DETR

Taylor, M and Cunningham, L (2001) *Constituting partnerships for neighbourhood renewal*, University of Brighton: Health and Social Policy Research Centre

Taylor, M. (2000) *Top down meets bottom up: Neighbourhood Management,* Joseph Rowntree Foundation

Teviot Community Plan (2000)

Magazine articles

Griffiths, J (2001) How smart businesses can lead the pack, *New Start*, Vol. 3, No. 109, p11

Lipman, C (2001) Nice of you to drop in, *New Start*, Vol. 3, No. 99, p12

Sanderson, I (2001) Evaluation needs to look at how initiatives work, *Urban Environment Today*, Issue 116, p14